THE SOFT
PADDLING
GUIDE

THE SOFT PADDLING GUIDE

To Ontario and New England

Jonathon Reynolds
and Heather Smith

The BOSTON
MILLS PRESS

Cataloguing in Publication Data

Reynolds, Jonathon, 1964-
   The soft paddling guide to Ontario and New England

ISBN 1-55046-335-7

1. Sea kayaking - New England - Guidebooks.
2. Sea kayaking - Ontario - Guidebooks.
3. Canoes and canoeing - New England - Guidebooks. 4. Canoes and canoeing - Ontario - Guidebooks. 5. New England - Guidebooks.
6. Ontario - Guidebooks.
I. Smith, Heather, 1969-   . II. Title.

GV776.N48R49 2001   797.1'224'0974
2001-930106-5

Published in 2001 by
Boston Mills Press
132 Main Street
Erin, Ontario N0B 1T0
Tel 519-833-2407
Fax 519-833-2195
e-mail books@bostonmillspress.com
www.bostonmillspress.com

An affiliate of
Stoddart Publishing Co. Limited
895 Don Mills Road
#400 2 Park Centre
Toronto, Ontario
Canada M3C 1W3
Tel 416-445-3333
Fax 416-445-5967
e-mail gdsinc@genpub.com

Distributed in Canada by
General Distribution Services Limited
325 Humber College Boulevard
Toronto, Canada M9W 7C3
Orders 1-800-387-0141 Ontario & Quebec
Orders 1-800-387-0172 NW Ontario
        & other provinces
e-mail customer.service@genpub.com

Distributed in the United States by
General Distribution Services Inc.
PMB 128, 4500 Witmer Industrial Estates
Niagara Falls, New York 14305-1386
Toll-free 1-800-805-1083
Toll-free fax 1-800-481-6207
e-mail gdsinc@genpub.com
www.genpub.com

Design by Mary Firth
Cover design by Gillian Stead
Text by Jonathon Reynolds
Photographs and maps by Jonathon Reynolds
   and Heather Smith
Printed in Canada

THE CANADA COUNCIL | LE CONSEIL DES ARTS
FOR THE ARTS | DU CANADA
SINCE 1957 | DEPUIS 1957

We acknowledge for their financial support of our publishing program the Canada Council, the Ontario Arts Council, and the Government of Canada through the Book Publishing Industry Development Program (BPIDP).

Contents

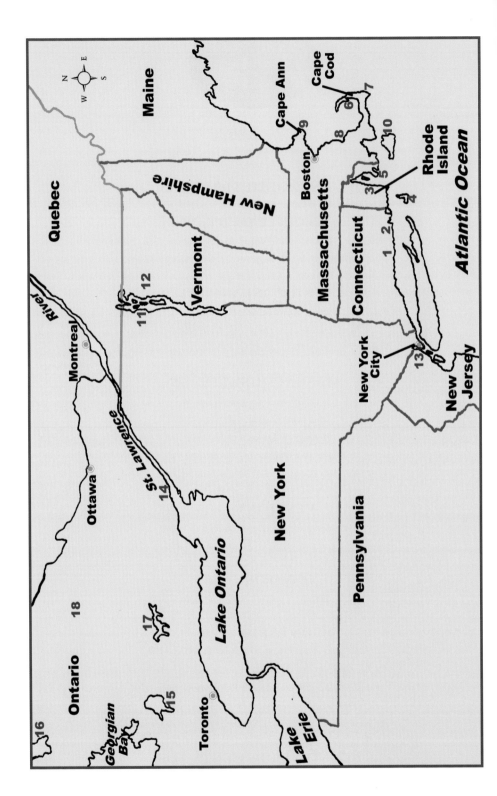

Introduction

Have you ever longed for a warm bed and a hot shower on a canoe or kayak trip? Then you will appreciate "soft paddling," a new approach to overnight paddling trips. Soft paddling is any paddling trip in which you stay at an inn or B&B instead of a campsite. It is a way of exploring waterways that are not in the wilderness and have no camping near them but offer unique or challenging paddling. Soft paddling also allows you to extend your paddling season into the spring and fall by providing warm, welcoming places to stay when the weather is too cold or miserable for comfortable camping.

Why soft? Soft on you, because you sleep in delightful inns and B&Bs. And soft on the planet, because you are accessing semi-wilderness and paddling areas close to home rather than traveling huge distances to get into the wilderness. Soft paddling doesn't necessarily mean "easy paddling" or that the areas featured here are not filled with wildlife and beauty. In fact, many of them are internationally recognized nature preserves.

The eighteen destinations singled out in this book are just a small fraction of the soft paddling options available in New England and Ontario. Each destination has been selected because it offers more than just a great place to paddle. Every spot has good paddling, remarkable natural or historical features, and a special place to sleep. In addition, each area has many off-the-water activities, so that a paddler can take a paddling vacation with a non-paddling partner and both parties will have lots to do.

Soft Paddling focuses on the top accommodations in each area featured and highlights the best paddling waters accessible from them. Just thinking about relaxing in a hot whirlpool bath, with a fine restaurant and a soft bed waiting, makes even the longest and coldest day of paddling seem much easier to take.

The waterways and coastline of New England and southern Ontario offer some incredibly beautiful paddling — some very sheltered and some very challenging — for paddlers of every skill level. *Soft Paddling* features eighteen destinations ranging from the cityscape of Manhattan to sea-kayaking waters on the New England coastline and canoeing wilderness lakes in Algonquin Park. Most waterways mentioned are most suitable for sea kayaking, but several trips are fine for canoeing as well. Each inn or B&B featured has been chosen to reflect the history and culture of its area. Each is unique to the destination — and they are all paddler friendly.

Choosing the inns and B&Bs to recommend in *Soft Paddling* was a long process. The star ratings Heather and I have given reflect more than just the standard of their accommodations. They also reflect ease of access to the water and the average price range. Four- and five-star inns will pamper you and give you ready access to superb paddling. If the featured inns are full or too expensive, you will find that many of the areas have other available accommodations nearby.

There are a few considerations for a soft paddling trip that are different from a camping trip with a kayak or a canoe. First of all, your wardrobe will need to include casual to dressy clothing as well as paddling gear. Many of the inns featured have dress codes for their dining rooms, so it's a good idea to check with the inn before you go to see what clothing would be appropriate.

Another item that would be very handy on most of these trips is a wheeled kayak cart. These come in many versions, but the best one for this type of travel is the kind that folds up to fit inside your kayak. I did manage to do all the trips described here without wheels for my kayak, but there were times when I would have greatly appreciated one, especially on the trips involving a ferry crossing.

Safety gear must also be part of your equipment when you go soft paddling. Even though these routes are daytrips, accidents do happen. You should always carry a set of dry clothes in a waterproof bag, a first aid kit, flares, a VHF radio (or cell phone in the areas with coverage), a map and compass, a spare paddle and paddle float, and, of course, the knowledge of how to use all of these items. Always wear a lifejacket. Make sure that you are appropriately dressed for the water and air temperature. Paddling in the spring and fall or on cold water makes you much more susceptible to hypothermia. You should always leave a float plan with someone who will miss you if you are late returning. Much of the paddling described here takes place on the ocean, where sudden changes in weather are common. Even if you are just planning a daytrip, be prepared for the worst and you will be fine. Make sure that the destination you have chosen has routes that are within your capabilities. Most destinations have areas that are safe for anyone to paddle in, but some waters should be tackled only by experienced paddlers. These spots are mentioned in the text of each chapter.

Finally, bring a sense of adventure and wonder to your vacation. Even though some of these destinations are very close to major population centers, they still allow you to see wildlife and experience natural beauty. These soft paddling trips will delight all of your senses, treating you to the smell of salt water, the sights of new surroundings, the taste of exquisite cuisine — and the luxury of a comfortable bed. Each of these eighteen very special places invites you to extend your paddling adventure with off-water explorations also.

CONNECTICUT

Essex and the Connecticut River: Nature and the "Gris"

E ssex is a pretty little town nestled on the banks of the Connecticut River. When you enter Essex it feels as if you are entering an earlier century. The village looks much as it did in the mid-1700s, except for the power lines, cars, and paved roads. The buildings have been meticulously restored, and there are no fast-food outlets or chain stores. First settled in 1648, Essex became a center for shipbuilding and international trade that thrived until the mid-1800s. In the late 1800s a sandbar that had formed across the mouth of the Connecticut River restricted large boat traffic on the river. All industrial development at the mouth of the river was halted. This was an economic disaster to the area at the time, and because of the depressed economy no real changes were made to the buildings in town for the next 100 years. It was a case of preservation through neglect. But in the past 50 years the local buildings have been restored, and the town now looks very well maintained. The river mouth has never been developed because shifting sandbars still make large craft navigation virtually impossible. As a result, the Connecticut River is the only major river in the United States that has virtually no development at the river mouth and is in a mostly natural state. It is a truly unique place to paddle.

The village of Essex is a center for pleasure boating and has been listed as the best small town in America. It is certainly one of the most charming small towns in Connecticut from which to paddle. Much of the land along the river has been set aside for conservation and habitat preservation. This area is an important wintering area for eagles and is a major stopover on the migration flyway for several species of birds. The combination of quaint village and riverside semi-wilderness makes this a wonderful soft paddling destination.

The Griswold Inn offers the only accommodations in town. The "Gris," as locals call it, opened for business in 1776. Sala Griswold, its first proprietor, promised "First Class Accommodations," and over 200 years later, the Griswold Inn is still offering first class accommodations. It is one of the oldest continuously operating inns in the United States. From the exterior, the inn looks like a conglomerate of buildings of various vintages joined together in one long rambling building. The main building is in fact made up of several buildings that have been moved to this spot at various times and added onto the main structure. The transported buildings include a covered bridge from New Hampshire and a schoolhouse from just down the street. Actually, the Gris comprises many other buildings in addition to the main inn building. All of them are linked together by the common white clapboard siding and the green shutters and accent trim.

The most recent owners, only the sixth since the inn opened, are the Paul brothers. They bought the inn in 1995 from William Winterer, and have restored much of it to its earlier glory as well as adding new bathrooms and other updates. The rooms are furnished in colonial antiques for the most part, and it is possible to imagine that you are being transported back in time when your room door closes behind you, shutting out all sounds from the street. The Griswold Inn feels like an old country inn, dignified yet personal, its very walls radiating the hospitality it has offered for more than two centuries.

The Griswold Inn is centrally located between three public water access points, all just a block away. The most private put-in is a small access point at the end of the road to the south, but it is not the easiest access because there is a gate at the end of the road. Straight down the road that the Griswold fronts on is a public launch ramp. This is the easiest put-in and take-out point.

Beside the launch ramp in the old 1878 steamboat warehouse is the Connecticut River Museum. It is now a warehouse of knowledge about the river and the history of boat traffic both large and small on the river. It is well worth taking the time to browse through this museum before you go paddling. The information that you pick up from looking through the exhibits and talking to the staff will make your paddle far more interesting. The museum also has children's programs that run in the summer, in case you want to bring the younger generation with you but don't want to take them paddling.

The wharf in front of the museum is called Steamboat Dock because for generations steamboats called in here on the run between New York City and Hartford, Connecticut. The put-in at Steamboat Dock is the easiest launch point in Essex, but in the summer months it can be quite busy, especially on weekends. The third access point is a public ramp one block north of the Gris. It leads directly into the waters surrounding the Essex Island Marina. Because this ramp will put you right into the marina, it is best used in the early spring and late fall when most boats are out of the water.

For all of these access points, it would be useful to have a kayak cart system. It is possible to carry boats the distance, but it is far easier to just wheel them down, and far, far easier to wheel them back after a long paddle. If you don't have

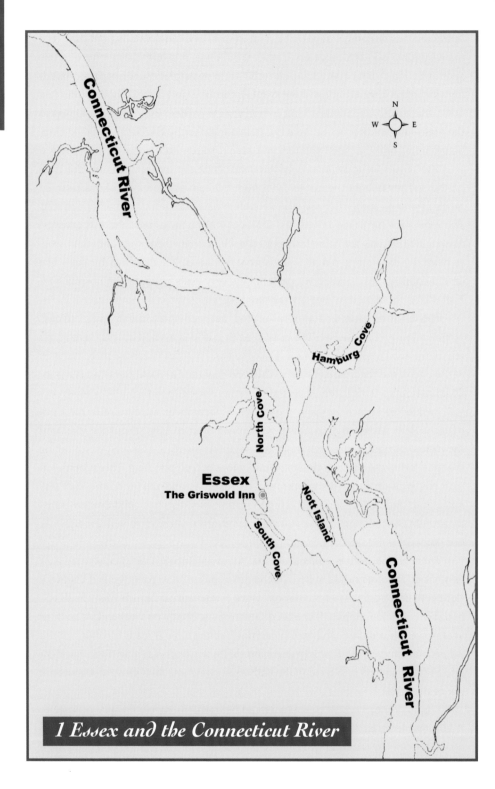

1 Essex and the Connecticut River

a wheel system, you could drive to each launch point and then return your vehicle to the inn. There is no parking at any of the put-in points.

The Connecticut River Estuary Regional Planning Council has published an excellent map of the Connecticut River Estuary Canoe/Kayak Trail. Actually, there are two such maps of paddling routes on the Connecticut River, but the most appropriate one for this area focuses on paddling out of the Town Park in Essex. These maps have interesting historical facts printed on them, and are laminated so that they are reasonably waterproof. You can pick them up at the Town Hall. (Ask at the front desk of the Gris for directions.)

In addition to seeing the local history, you can observe an abundance of wildlife from the water on the Connecticut River. For a nature lover this is an excellent paddling destination. Much of the land near the mouth of the river and in the estuary is controlled by the Nature Conservancy and so will never be developed. This land is home to many different types of animals and thousands of birds. The best times for wildlife viewing on the river are the early morning and late evening, and the best seasons are spring and fall. Boat traffic is only prevalent from late May until early September, and in the summer months it is much lighter during the week than on weekends.

If you plan your paddle to coincide with the tides, you can get the tidal current to help you upstream and then drift back on the ebb tide and the natural river current. Even if you can't use the tides to your advantage, it is possible to plan a route through the coves and islands around Essex so that you don't spend too much energy fighting a current. To the immediate south of town is Middle Cove, which is bounded on the south by Thatchbed Island. As its name implies, Thatchbed Island is very grassy and the water close to it is quite shallow. There are generally several beautiful boats moored in Middle Cove; these are very pretty when seen from the waterline, as are the beautiful homes lining the shore.

It is possible to slip between Thatchbed Island and the Mainland into South Cove. At low tide this is quite tricky due to the sand beds along the shore of the island and the mainland. South Cove seems wilder and more natural than Middle Cove, and the further into the cove you get, the fewer homes are visible from the water. As you leave South Cove and enter the main channel of the Connecticut River you will pass Hayden's Point on your right.

While I was paddling along the steep shoreline south of Hayden's Point, I saw a small red fox stalk and catch a squirrel. Because I was on the water and drifting with the ebb tide, I was completely silent. So I was able to watch the fox for about twenty minutes as he trotted down the beach with the squirrel in his mouth and made frequent stops to eat, with only his ears sticking up from behind the driftwood logs on the beach.

As you cut across the main channel to the southern tip of Nott Island, you will begin to see many different species of birds. The southern tip of Nott Island is so low that it looks as if it is in danger of sinking, but it provides a wonderful bird habitat. On my paddle, I saw hundreds of birds ranging from small swallows with iridescent blue feathers to majestic swans gliding among the reeds. I also saw deer on the island. Much of the mainland on the eastern shore here is preserved land and has a real wild feel with no visible development apart from a few birdwatching blinds.

Heading upriver from Nott Island, you have a choice of continuing up the main channel to Brockway Island and the cliffs below Selden Neck State Park or heading back across the main channel into North Cove. If you paddle to the east of Brockway Island you will find Hamburg Cove, a sheltered deep-water cove surrounded by wooded slopes with slices of granite cliffs showing through the trees. It has quite a different topography from the marshland and coastal estuary further south.

As you leave Hamburg Cove and cross the river north of Brockway Island to the east shore, you will approach a long flat, wide peninsula called Great Meadow, which extends downriver from the western shore. This great grassy area was once harvested for hay for livestock bedding but now it is a nesting place for thousands of birds. Great Meadow forms the eastern boundary of North Cove, which is where you would have ended up if you had continued across the river from Nott Island.

Extending from the southern tip of Great Meadow almost into the town of Essex is Essex Island. The channel at the south end of the island can be extremely busy with boat traffic since it cuts directly between the Essex Island Marina and another fair-sized marina. Be extremely careful paddling through this area. A far better access point into North Cove is the tiny channel at the north end of Essex Island. This channel is so shallow at low tide that only a kayak or a canoe could get through it, so very little boat traffic passes by.

As you paddle through the channel you will see the Riverview Cemetery directly in front of you and across the cove. This is the oldest cemetery in Essex and, along with a windmill, now a residence, right beside it, provides an excellent navigation point for paddling in this area. Eagles can sometimes be spotted here during late fall or early spring paddling, since they winter over in the lower Connecticut River valley.

Paddling northward up North Cove, you will eventually come to a condominium complex on the west shore. This marks the entrance to Falls River Cove. The swans that glide among the reeds give this quiet waterway a romantic quality. Falls River Cove extends westward for a few thousand feet and is bordered by beautiful homes with lovely gardens that spill down the slope to the water. These quiet homes give no indication that a thriving shipbuilding business was once located here along with several mills and other businesses.

In early spring 1814, the British raided Essex and burned twenty-eight ships. But they spared the town and used the Griswold Inn as their headquarters. The menu of the Sunday morning Hunt Breakfast, similar to the meal the British demanded during their occupation of the Griswold, has been served ever since. If you are looking for a good big meal to give you lots of reserve energy to paddle on, the Hunt Breakfast will give you a great start.

After a day on the water, you will want to return to the Griswold Inn to clean up and then think about where to have dinner. You really only have two choices in Essex unless you want to drive. The food at the Griswold is excellent, and they offer quite a variety with an emphasis on country and New England fare. Eating in-house also gives you the advantage of being close to your room if you are really tired from all that paddling.

A short walk downtown will take you to the Black Seal. This small pub/restaurant serves good simple meals and is less expensive than the Griswold. The atmosphere at the Black Seal is definitely nautical, with ropes and block and tackle hanging from the ceiling and pictures of ships on the walls. This is a very busy restaurant, so be prepared to wait for a table or go early to avoid the rush.

If you decide to have a meal at the Griswold, you have a choice of six dining rooms. The food is the same in all of them — superb — but the atmosphere ranges from the small, quite casual Gun Room to the large, more formal Covered Bridge Room. All of the walls are decorated with prints and memorabilia collected over the last two centuries. There is always something fascinating to look at between courses.

After dinner and before you head to bed, you may want to check out the Tap Room. The tavern at the Griswold has been much the same since it was moved here by a team of oxen late in the eighteenth century. Originally built as a schoolhouse in 1738, the Tap Room is now steeped in the tradition of a centuries-old pub. It features live music every night, ranging from sea chanteys to jazz or banjo music. The walls are completely covered with pictures of ships and other nautical artifacts. The original plaster ceiling made with horsehair and crushed seashells curves up overhead, its aged patina almost glossy in appearance. A large potbellied stove dominates the center of the room with its stovepipe angling across the room to the chimney over the large fireplace. Two long oars from the whaler *Charles M. Morgan* hang from the sprinkler system pipes, and you are served at a bar carved from wood in the Gothic style. A couple of drinks while listening to centuries-old sea chanteys will take you back a few hundred years to a different era. It is a fitting way to end a day on the water.

If you want to extend your stay at the Griswold for more than a few nights, you will find several additional excellent paddling destinations within a short drive. It is also an option to paddle right out into Long Island Sound from Essex, but it would be a long return trip. If you have two vehicles, you could drive upstream and spend a leisurely day paddling south from East Haddam. This would also give you a chance to explore Gillette Castle, a castle built by an eccentric actor who became famous for his portayal of Sherlock Holmes. Gillette Castle is now a State Park.

Old Lyme, on the eastern shore of the Connecticut River just at the mouth of the river, has another Connecticut River Estuary Canoe/Kayak Trail route through the tidal marshes there. If you are a birdwatcher and enjoy paddling through tidal marshland in search of new birds, this is an area not to be missed. The Connecticut River Estuary Regional Planning Agency has published an excellent map of this area for paddlers.

Essex has a wide variety of activities for days when you either can't or don't want to paddle. You could easily spend a day just exploring the area on foot or by bike. Biking to Chester or Deep River alongside the Connecticut River and back to Essex is a wonderful way to spend a day. If you are looking for a guided tour of the area, you could set one up with the CT Audubon Society EcoTravel office, located at the foot of Main Street just a block from the Griswold Inn. They offer local tours and know this area inside out.

There are three museums in Essex: the Pratt House, open only on summer weekends; the Museum of Fife and Drum in nearby Ivoryton; and, of course, the Connecticut River Museum, also just a block from the Griswold Inn. For a more interactive history adventure, try out the Essex Steam Train. You can ride on a historic train up the river valley to Chester with the possible option of a steamboat cruise in Deep River. For those of you looking to own a bit of history, there are several antique shops in Essex Village.

There are also a few theaters in the local area. The historic Ivoryton Playhouse, the country's oldest self-supporting playhouse, hosts arts events throughout the year. Situated across the river (cross by ferry) and a bit further north are the Goodspeed Opera House, Gillette Castle near the village of East Haddam on the east side of the Connecticut River, and the lovely villages of Chester and Deep River, complete with their antique shops and tiny boutiques on the west side of the river. The Griswold Inn has a booklet that details three local walks of various distances.

Essex and the Connecticut River

INN INFO

The Griswold Inn ★★★★
36 Main Street
Essex, CT 06426
860-767-1776
Fax: 860-767-0481
www.griswoldinn.com
griswoldinn@snet.net

LOCAL CONTACTS

Essex Village Website at http://essex.com for links to local sites and information on paddling and local tides.

Connecticut Audubon Society EcoTravel
67 Main St.
Essex, CT 06426
800-996-8747
860-767-0660
E-mail: CTAUDUBON@AOL.COM

Connecticut River Museum
860-767-8269
E-mail: crm@connix.com
For more information about the children's programs, contact the education director at 860-767-8269. They fill up quickly, so call well ahead.

Essex Steam Train
860-767-0103

Museum of Fife & Drum
860-767-2237

Ivoryton Playhouse
860-767-7318

MAPS & CHARTS

Connecticut River maps available at the Essex Town Hall.
NOAA # 12373 at 1:20,000

RENTALS

Black Hall Marina
(rents canoes and kayaks, just across the river in Old Lyme, mid-May to mid-September)
132 Shore Road
Old Lyme, CT 06371
P.O. Box 261
860-434-9680

TRAVEL INFO

Essex is most easily reached by car, and kayak rentals in this area are far enough from water that you'll need a car to transport your boat to the inn. Once at the inn, you won't need a car until you are ready to leave.

Mystic River and Mystic Seaport:
A Paddle Back in Time

Mystic Seaport is one of the premier maritime museums in the world with almost 500 vessels and a huge 17-acre historic village at the banks of the Mystic River. Mystic Seaport the museum is just upstream from the town of Mystic.

The town of Mystic is an old fishing and boatbuilding town that is now devoted almost totally to tourism. It is split by the Mystic River, with most of the downtown shops lined along Bridge Street. It is a delightful little seaport town to wander around but the real attraction in Mystic is Mystic Seaport. Started on Christmas Eve in 1929 by three local citizens who were concerned about the loss of their marine heritage, Mystic Seaport is now the largest maritime museum in the world, with over 300 full-time employees. It is constantly expanding and evolving, with their latest large project being a decade long exhibition called "Voyages" that documents the role of boats and boating in American history and culture. Each year they focus on a different area of history and showcase it at Mystic Seaport Village. It takes far more than one day to explore all that Mystic Seaport has to offer, especially for those of us who love old boats and ships.

One of the best ways I can think of to get a sense of the proportions of Mystic Seaport and truly appreciate the wide range of boats moored here, from simplest rowing craft to ocean-going schooners, is to paddle around the shore in a kayak. Once you have paddled around the waterline of the tall ships you will have a greater appreciation for their size when you later explore them from land.

I chose Six Broadway Inn, a beautifully restored B&B, as the best location to stay while in Mystic because of its close proximity to Mystic Seaport and to the public access points on the river. The best spot to put in is just south of the shipyard at Mystic Seaport, at the end of Isham Street. This public ramp is about four blocks from Six Broadway Inn.

It is possible to carry your kayak there, and if you have a folding kayak cart, then you'll easily be able to walk over to the put-in. It is also possible to drive and park alongside the road leading down to the ramp, but parking is at a premium and your chances of finding a spot are not good, especially in the summer. If you can't carry your boat over and there are two of you, it would be best to drive over and drop your kayaks off. One of you can then return the car to the inn and quickly walk back to the put-in point — about a five-minute walk alongside the river.

This section of the river is tidal, so the direction you set out in will be determined by the direction of the tides. It is of course possible to paddle against the tides here since they are not all that strong, but I figure why work more than you have to?

If you paddle north from the Isham Street launch ramp, you are immediately enveloped by the mystery of Mystic Seaport. The pier that runs out into the water just north of the launch ramp is the shipyard pier for Mystic Seaport. The last time I paddled there, a replica of the schooner *Amistad* was being fitted out with rigging and spars. This reproduction was being constructed at Mystic Seaport shipyard to commemorate the revolt of a group of enslaved Africans being transported from Sierra Leone on a ship much like it. The prisoners overpowered their captors and were picked up off the coast of Long Island. Eventually, in a landmark decision after a long series of trials, they were freed and allowed to return to their homeland. The *Amistad* is now a floating classroom and exhibit that travels throughout the United States.

Paddling around the end of the shipyard pier and into the heart of the shoreline of Mystic Seaport's historic village is like paddling back into history. Tall masts

Step back in time as you wander through the streets of Mystic Seaport Museum.

CONNECTICUT

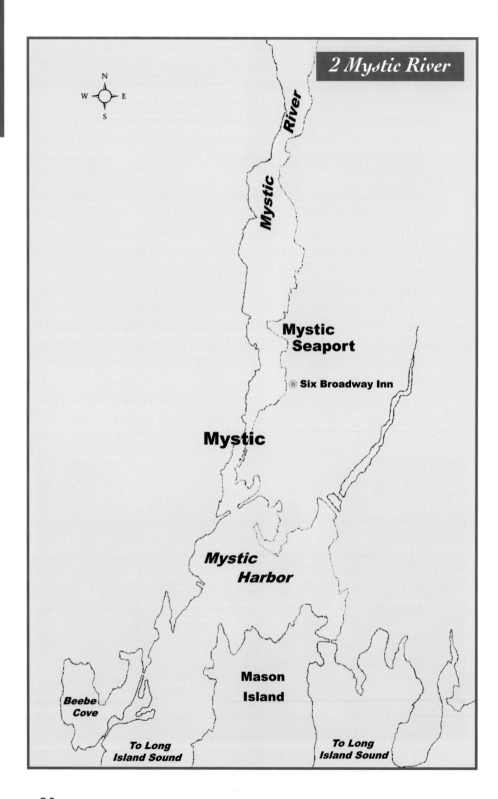

2 Mystic River

N
W E
S

Mystic River

Mystic Seaport

◉ Six Broadway Inn

Mystic

Mystic Harbor

Beebe Cove

Mason Island

To Long Island Sound

To Long Island Sound

pierce the sky and dozens of smaller sailing craft line the docks. Upstream from you, Lighthouse Point juts out into the river forming two coves, one on either flank of the point. Each of these coves is lined with docks at which a huge variety of vessels are moored, some permanent and some transient. The huge schooner *L.A. Dunton* is moored at the long pier at the center of the first cove.

The longest ship at Mystic Seaport, the *L.A. Dunton* spent a long productive life as a fishing schooner before it found a home here teaching us about our past. On the other side of the same pier is the steamboat *Sabino,* which holds the distinction of being the oldest operating steam ferry in the United States. The long, low dock south of the *L.A. Dunton* is where the local rowing club members land and launch their rowing shells. If you are lucky you will see these graceful and sleek craft flying up the river. The best time to see them is the late afternoon or early morning when the wind is calmest.

As you paddle on up the shoreline, you will have to thread your way through other moored and anchored boats. Just before you reach the end of the point and the lighthouse, you will see a large open-sided building on the shore. This is the boatshed, where classes in boatbuilding are held, including one on building a skin kayak. It is not legal for you to land without a ticket, and it might not be safe to leave your kayak on the shore here in any case. But you can always come back from the land side another time and fully explore the areas that looked the most intriguing from the water.

As you round Lighthouse Point, you will see the masts of the *Joseph Conrad* behind the youth training building. There are usually several small sailing dinghies sailing around markers off the docks in front of this facility. Keep a weather eye out for novice sailors since they may not have complete control of their vessels. The *Joseph Conrad* is a tall ship that dwarfs a kayak. It is an interesting experiment in perspective and proportion to paddle around such large ships in a kayak. If you lean back in the kayak, you can see the yardarms hanging far out over the side of the ship. Just thinking about hanging out on one of those upper yardarms in a winter gale makes me shiver even on a warm sunny day

Past the *Joseph Conrad* is Middle Wharf, which has a constantly changing roster of boats, and behind that is the *Charles W. Morgan,* the last of the wooden Yankee whalers. This is not the most elegant ship, nor was its mission, but it is a fine example of an American wooden sailing whaler. The *Morgan* is moored to Chubbs Wharf, which divides the public boats of Mystic Seaport Museum from the private yachts moored in the next basin. While I was there I met a family from New Zealand who had been cruising for five years. Needless to say, I was a bit jealous.

Mystic Seaport might be the main reason to paddle the Mystic River, but it is by no means the only one. Past the historical village, the river widens out into a

Spring is a very colorful time to visit Mystic Seaport.

larger basin area that extends north for a mile (2 km) or so. Just after it narrows down, the river passes under Interstate 95. The roar of trucks racing overhead seems strangely out of place during a paddle along an otherwise tranquil river. Past the highway bridge, the river widens out again into a broad pond-like area with a few marshy sections along the shoreline. The farther north you paddle, the more birds you are likely to see. The marshy shoreline and small number of homes make it feel as if you are much farther away from people than you actually are.

Rounding the last bit of river, with the current getting quite strong, you will see the buildings of Old Mystic. As its name implies, this fishing and whaling port was settled before Mystic, but the coming of the railway and the need for a deep-water harbor meant that it went into decline, and it never got much larger than it is right now. Just past Old Mystic, the river becomes too rocky and shallow even for kayaks to keep going, and it's time to turn around and head back downstream to Mystic and a nice relaxing evening at Six Broadway Inn.

Six Broadway Inn is an 1854 Victorian home that has been painstaking restored and renovated by Jerry Sullivan, your host. He has personally done most of the work on the house and has poured a lot of himself into the place. Six Broadway Inn is ideally located in Mystic. It is a short walk to the downtown section of Mystic and a ten-minute walk away from the front gates of Mystic Seaport Museum. Most important for those of us who paddle, it is just a five-minute walk from the best kayak launch site in Mystic. There is ample parking — and even a spot to rinse off your kayak and gear after a day's paddle. The rooms are all furnished with period antiques and have great bathrooms. Breakfast is served in the breakfast room or, if the weather permits, on the gazebo deck. This inn tends to book up quickly, so reserve well in advance for weekends or summer trips.

Another day, you may plan to paddle south from the put-in at Isham Street. Heading south from the put-in point will take you through the town of Mystic and out onto Long Island Sound. Boat traffic can be very intense, especially after you pass under the swing bridge, since large marinas line both sides of the river mouth here. Examples of almost every type of recreational boat imaginable are docked at these marinas.

Follow the signs down through the channel and you will find yourself on the more open water of Mystic Harbor. Mason Island, which is joined to the mainland by a bridge on the far eastern edge, shelters this harbor very well. But once you are out from behind the protective presence of Mason Island, you will be exposed to the winds funneling down Long Island Sound. It is still quite a protected paddle, however, due to the location of Fishers Island a couple of miles (3 km) offshore. Fishers Island is private, so it is not a good destination for a paddle.

A circumnavigation of Mason Island is an excellent day- or half-day trip, depending on how much time you spend exploring the little coves and inlets in the island and on the mainland coast. Try to time your return into the Mystic River with the incoming tide so that you won't have to fight the current. Once again, take care around the boat traffic near the marinas and under the bridge.

Mystic has many off-water activities in addition to Mystic Seaport Museum. The Mystic Aquarium, a ten-minute drive from Six Broadway Inn, is an excellent place to spend a rainy day. The aquarium's forty-eight exhibits include over 6,000 living specimens of sea life, from coral reefs to jellyfish and colonies of penguins, as well as interactive experiences of the technology and challenges of deep-sea exploration. Regular shows featuring whales, dolphins, and sea lions take place in its large indoor marine theater.

Another great way to spend a bad-weather day is to visit the Mashantucket Pequot Museum and Research Center. This museum showcases the history and prehistory of the local Native Americans. Touted as one of the best interactive museums in the state, this museum allows you to meet a giant mastodon and you can watch an ancient caribou hunt happen in front of you. The interactive nature of the displays and the live performances in the museum make this a more personal visit than most museum trips. You can also explore a 400-year-old Indian village, populated by more than fifty life-size figures, that brings the history of the local natives back to life.

Mystic River and Mystic Seaport

INN INFO

Six Broadway Inn ★ ★ ★
6 Broadway Ave.
Mystic, CT 06355
Tel. & fax: 860-536-6010
1-888-44MYSTIC or
1-888-446-9784
www.visitmystic.com/sixbroadway

LOCAL CONTACTS

Mystic Aquarium
55 Coogan Boulevard
Mystic, CT 06355
860-572-5955

Masantucket Pequot Museum and Research Center
110 Pequot Trail
P.O. Box 3180
Mashantucket, CT 06339
1-800-411-9671

MAPS & CHARTS

NOAA # 13214 at 1:20,000

RENTALS

Mystic River Kayak, Bike & Moped Rentals/Tours
18A Holmes Street
Mystic, CT 06355
860-536- 8381
(rents Old Town Loons)

TRAVEL INFO

Mystic can be reached by plane, train, and car.

TRAIN

Several **Amtrak** trains stop each day in Mystic from Boston (about 2 hours) and New York (about 2.5 hours). For departure times, call Amtrak at 1-800-872-7245.

PLANE

The **Groton–New London Airport** is roughly 8 miles (13 km) from Mystic, with several flights to and from New York. You can also get to Mystic from larger airports such as Bradley Airport in Hartford, CT, about 2 hours away.

RHODE ISLAND

Paddling Wickford, Narragansett Bay, and Ninigret Pond

Arriving in Wickford, Rhode Island, is like stepping back 200 years. This is a tranquil seaside village originally surveyed in 1707 by Lodowick Updike under the name Updike's Newtown. It is said that the novel *The Witches of Eastwick,* by Wickford's most famous resident, novelist John Updike, was based on life in this village. Much of the architecture of this classic, small New England town dates from the late Revolutionary and early Federal period. The more modern buildings in town blend with the old in a comfortable evolution of styles.

Wickford was originally built on an island, and although the village is now firmly attached to the mainland, some local people still call it the "Venice of New England," due to the waterways surrounding and running through the town. The sea still provides much of its economic base, and the town prides itself on being a living residential and commercial village, not primarily a seasonal tourist attraction. The main street is lined with antique shops, gift shops and a surprising number of good restaurants for a village this size.

Exploring Wickford's waterways by kayak is a great way to see a different side of this area. The paddling options described here cover more than just the Wickford Harbor, so a car is necessary to completely experience the different types of paddling that this section of Rhode Island has to offer. In case you do not have a kayak of your own, Rhode Island's biggest paddle-sports center, the Kayak Centre, located in Wickford, could help you out. The Kayak Centre also has a rental facility on Ninigret Pond, a wildlife refuge that is the other main paddling area featured in this chapter.

It is possible to chose from a wide range of accommodations, many in historic homes in the local area, and not have to worry about water access since the rental centers are right on the water at both sites. For those of you with your own kayaks, there are public launch spots in both places as well. When you arrive in Wickford, ask at the Kayak Centre where the best launch site is. Conditions and access points change, and the staff at the Kayak Centre will have the latest information.

Wickford Cove has an active commercial fishing fleet as well as dozens of pleasure craft and tall sailing yachts. Each part of the harbor is home to a different type of vessel. The commercial fishing boats dock off the west shore closest to the old town, while the pleasure boats line the docks along the east shore. The pleasure boats even seem to be sorted according to whether they are sailboats or motor-boats. The motorboats tend to be docked closest to shore and the sailboats further out at the end of the piers and docks. In a long line, following the channel through the Z-shaped harbor, the sailboats with the deepest draft are moored to clusters or pilings driven deep in the bottom of the harbor.

Running west out of the cove is a river channel that will take you under a bridge and into calm water. There are often swans or geese on the ponds here, and you will paddle by folks dining at the waterside restaurants. Returning under the bridge to the water of the cove, it is best to keep close to the western shore. The water is quite shallow here, so no boats other than kayaks can travel through here. At low tide, however, even kayaks will have a problem bumping and grinding along the shell-encrusted bottom.

Leaving Wickford Cove past the fishy-smelling commercial docks, you will enter the larger basin of Wickford Harbor. To the east, long breakwaters extend from the north and south into the water. To the west is the channel leading to Mill Cove. The direction you turn will depend largely on what the weather is like and the type of paddling experience you want to have. For sheltered gentle paddling and birdwatching, turn west; for open water and the possibility of seeing seals, turn east. We will go west first and then come back and follow the route east out into the West Passage of Narragansett Bay.

Mill Cove extends through a channel between Cornelius Island on the north and the Wickford shoreline on the south. The north-facing Wickford shoreline is defined by two points with a narrow bay sandwiched between them. The shores of Wharf Point, the bay, and Cedar Tree Point are encrusted with docks and marinas. The water offshore is cluttered with mooring buoys and dozens of different types of craft. Just past Cedar Tree Point is another narrow waterway running deep into the center of Wickford. Long Point, on the west side of this passage, has a public launch ramp that paddlers with their own boats may want to use.

Mill Cove continues on in three directions once you pass Long Point, but only one of these will take you very far. If you head north, you will enter the mouth of Mill Creek, which twists and turns, winding its way through marsh and wooded shoreline to finally end in a maze of channels an hour's paddle north of Mill Cove. Along the way you will see wood ducks, herons, grebes, and many other common waterfowl. Navigation here is very easy, and there are no difficult sections in this paddle. On your return to Mill Cove, consider paddling around

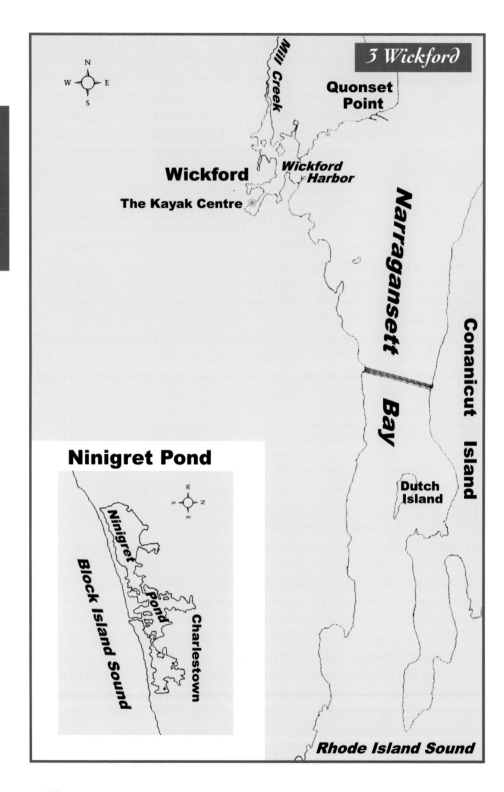

3 Wickford

Mill Creek

Quonset Point

Wickford

Wickford Harbor

The Kayak Centre

Narragansett Bay

Conanicut Island

Dutch Island

Ninigret Pond

Ninigret Pond

Block Island Sound

Charlestown

Rhode Island Sound

Cornelius Island into Fishing Cove if you have the energy and time. This large, shallow cove offers a respite from the busy channel that services the marinas all along the shore of Wickford.

Paddling east out of Wickford Harbor you will pass between the ends of the two long breakwaters. Once through the gap in these walls you will be out on Narragansett Bay. To the south you will see the shoreline slant eastward, and in the distance a high bridge leaps across the water on tall legs. Eastward, the tip of Conanicut Island appears, about two and a half miles (4 km) away. To the north, the huge Quonset Point complex dominates the horizon. This was once one of the huge military bases that dot Rhode Island. This one gave its name to the most common of military buildings, the corrugated metal Quonset hut, but now the base lies mostly empty. Quonset Point was the base for the search and investigation of the Egypt Air crash off the coast here in 1999. There is very little reason to paddle north here since the former base is not the prettiest of places. An ideal destination for a long day paddle would be Dutch Island, about a mile (2 km) south of the high bridge linking the mainland to Conanicut Island.

The western shore south of Wickford Harbor has three nubs of land thrusting eastward. Between these small peninsulas are shallow bays filled with anchored boats. A person at a Rhode Island State tourism office told me that Narragansett Bay has more boats per square mile than any other body of water in the United States. If you paddle here on a weekend you will believe that statement. However, on weekdays and in the spring and fall it is possible to feel as if you have the entire bay to yourself.

Harbor Fox Island lies just offshore about a mile (2 km) south of Wickford. This island is private, so you can't land, but sometimes seals pull themselves out of the water to sun themselves on the rocks here. They are very shy, so be quiet when paddling up to the island. Continuing south, you will see that the outline of the bridge splits into two bridges. The new bridge was built beside the old bridge that now is abandoned and closed to traffic. Local rumor has it that the old bridge is for sale. I am not quite sure what you could use it for but if you want a bridge it is here for whoever can afford it. Another local fisherman said that the old bridge was going to be destroyed and yet another said it was going to be turned into part of the bike route around Rhode Island. What ever the real story is, paddling under these bridges makes you feel very small.

There is a small light tower right in the middle of the channel, dwarfed by the bridges. Check the tidal current when you paddle past this tower or past the huge concrete piers. Ideally, you will be paddling down to Dutch Island on an ebb tide and returning on a flood tide. This will give you time to have a picnic lunch on Dutch Island at low tide and save you the trouble of fighting a current both ways.

Swans and fishermen share the waters of Wickford with kayakers.

The tidal current here runs at about one knot, but it can seem like much more in shallower areas or where the channel narrows.

The north shore of Dutch Island is lined with bluffs, but at the southern tip there is a good landing area. Dutch Island houses a simple square lighthouse and some concrete ruins. The lighthouse became operational in 1857 and was constantly manned until 1947 when it was automated. In 1979 the light was deactivated, and the 42-foot-tall brick tower is now empty. The concrete foundations scattered around the island date from the 1940s, but now the island is uninhabited so it makes a great lunch spot and turn-around point.

From the south end of Dutch Island you can see the open water of Rhode Island Sound and past that clear out into the Atlantic Ocean. With a south or east wind, the ocean swells reach up to Dutch Island, gently pushing you back to Wickford. As you paddle back north, the huge former military base dominates the northern horizon. Before you get to Quonset Point, though, the entrance to Wickford Harbor opens up on the western shore, and you paddle back to your waiting car or to the Kayak Centre to return your kayak.

For another excursion, you could take the twenty-minute drive from Wickford to the shore of Ninigret Pond. Access is either via Charlestown Beach Road to the

Charlestown Breachway or via East Beach Road to East Beach. The Kayak Centre rental location is on the Charlestown Beach Road just before the bridge that carries the road over the channel connecting Green Pond and Ninigret Pond. Much of the western half of Ninigret Pond is a wildlife refuge: the Ninigret National Wildlife Refuge, the Ninigret Conservation Area, the Frosty Drew Observatory, and the Ningret State Park and State Beach all add to the wilderness protection.

Ninigret Pond is a must-paddle destination for any birdwatcher. The large areas of protected marsh combined with the food rich environments make this saltwater pond a birder's paradise, especially in the spring and fall. Many migrating birds use Ninigret as a safe stopover on the long flight north in the spring or south in the fall. The vibrant red, orange, and yellow foliage, in combination with crisp air — and no bugs — are added attractions in the fall.

There is no best route to paddle in Ninigret Pond. I recommend exploring without any real plan, instead of following a route. Know how long you have and where you are on the pond at all times so that you know you can get back when you plan to. It is possible to paddle into Green Pond from Ninigret and up north into Fort Neck Pond as well. The best wildlife viewing is at the western end of the pond. Do not land in the National Wildlife area. But it is possible to land on the back side of East Beach and walk over to see the waves crashing in on the shore.

The only area of concern in the entire pond is the Charlestown Breachway. The tidal currents running through this breachway can be very, very strong, throwing up standing waves and creating nasty undercurrents. Unless you have good whitewater paddling skills, stay away from the breachway. The rest of the pond is quite benign — the biggest hazard you are likely to encounter would be an out-of-control windsurfer. It can take several hours to completely explore Ninigret Pond, so plan on taking lots of time.

Wickford, Narragansett Bay, and Ninigret Pond

INN INFO

Wickford is a delightful town to wander around in when you are off the water and it has several excellent B&Bs. Check with the North Kingston Chamber of Commerce. The Ocean Rose Inn is located about halfway between Wickford and Ninigret Pond. It is ideally located between Ninigret Pond and Wickford.

Ocean Rose Inn
113 Ocean Road
Narragansett, RI
401-783-4704
www.oceanroseinn.com

North Kingstown Chamber of Commerce
8045 Post Road
North Kingstown, RI 02852
401-295-5566
Fax: 401-295-5582
E-mail: info@northkingstown.com
www.northkingstown.com

MAPS & CHARTS

Available at the Kayak Centre.
Waterproof Charts, # 27

RENTALS

The Kayak Centre
9 Philips St. Waterside
Wickford, RI 02852
Tel: 401-295-4400
1-888-SEA-KAYAK
1-888-732-5292
www.kayakcentre.com
fun@kayakcentre.com

TRAVEL INFO

You will need a car to access most of the paddling featured here.

Rhode Island can be reached in a couple of hours from Boston and about four hours from New York. This tiny state is full of paddling options — only a few of them are explored in this book.

Block Island: Open Ocean and Idyllic Retreat

Block Island is a small island about 12 miles (20 km) off the Rhode Island coast in Long Island Sound. It was originally called Manisses, or Island of the Little God, by the local Natives, but was later named "Block Island" after a Dutch navigator, Adriaen Block. The first European settlers came in 1661 seeking religious freedom, and they established a fishing- and farming-based community that is still very evident today. This small island — it is less than 11 square miles (28 hectares) in size — has a barren, windswept character that is compensated for by long sand beaches, a charming village, and wonderful paddling.

Block Island is an ideal destination for paddlers who also love hiking because the entire island is crisscrossed with hiking trails and everything is within walking distance. Bicycling is an even quicker way to get around, and you can easily explore most of the island in a day or two. This is also an excellent destination for avid birders especially in the spring and fall when migrating birds stop over on their long flights. But the main reason to come here is the ocean — and for paddlers, paddling on that ocean.

Block Island is fully exposed to the Atlantic, with all its power. Its waters require more commitment than mainland waters, and the weather here can change very quickly. One beautiful sunny spring day, for example, I was paddling along the eastern shore just north of Old Harbor. The horizon was a bit obscured by mist, and out of habit I was regularly checking my compass bearing. But the shore was only a couple of hundred yards to my left, so I felt quite relaxed. I stopped to take some pictures (unsuccessfully) of a grebe just off my starboard bow.

When I looked up from stowing my camera ten minutes later, I could no longer see the shoreline. I could still hear the waves crashing on the beach but that sound was becoming muted as well. As I watched the wall of mist envelope me even the bow of my kayak became blurry, and the temperature seemed to drop several degrees in a brief minute. I looked at my compass, noticed that I had fallen off my heading by a few degrees, and quickly corrected my course. For the next forty-

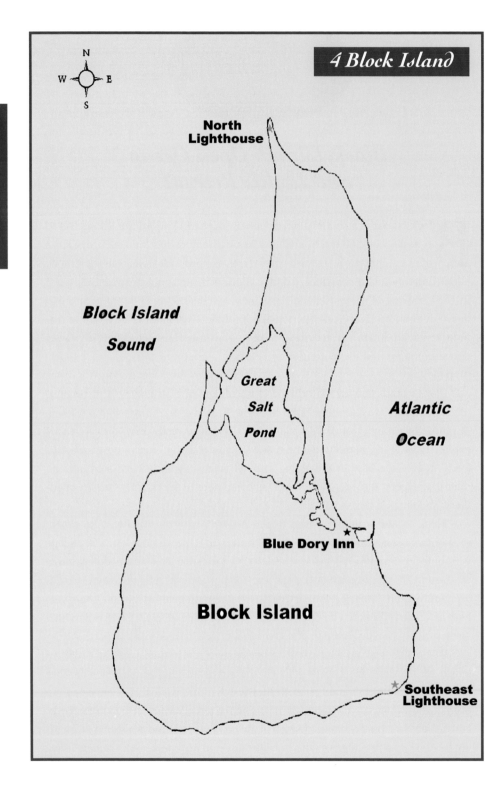

N
W E
S

North
Lighthouse

Block Island

Sound

Great

Salt

Pond

Atlantic

Ocean

Blue Dory Inn

Block Island

Southeast
Lighthouse

five minutes of paddling the only reference points I had were my compass heading and the by now very faint sounds of surf crashing on the beach.

I had plenty of time to think about the fact that if I got off course the next land eastward was on the other side of the Atlantic Ocean. Heading south I might hit Cuba or the Bahamas, but there was not much chance of that either. I kept heading north. When the sun eventually burned off the fog, I was relieved to see the gravel cliffs that line the northeastern part of the island on my left. Remember this when you are planning your day's paddle off Block Island. The closest bit of mainland is 12 miles (20 km) away, and the distances go up exponentially after that.

Along with the sudden changes in weather there are tidal currents and rips to be concerned about when paddling along the shores of Block Island. At the northern tip, around Sandy Point, the tidal currents clash and create a spectacular and quite dangerous riptide. Two sets of waves meet almost head on, throwing spray high into the air. Don't paddle off Sandy Point unless you are a very experienced paddler, and even then take all the precautions you can. The best way to view the riptide clash at Sandy Point is to cycle out to Chaqum Pond and hike out to North Light, a granite lighthouse dating from 1867, which now houses a maritime museum and interpretive center.

Block Island is almost cut in half by Great Salt Pond. This huge, very sheltered anchorage empties into the ocean on the western shore of Block Island through a manmade cut, and comes within a couple of hundred yards of the innermost curve of Crescent Beach on the eastern shore of the island. Using this short distance as a portage makes it possible to paddle around the southern half of the island and avoid tackling the northern point with the dangerous rip currents there. Crescent Beach, just north of Old Harbor, is an ideal starting point for a paddle around the southern half of Block Island. A word of warning, though. There are very few safe landing spots on the southern shore, so be prepared for a few hours in your boat before you leave.

At the south end of Crescent Beach, there are several rocks just offshore. They break up any swell that comes into the beach, making for an easy launch. From the beach, paddle out around the breakwaters protecting Old Harbor and the ferry dock, and head south along the shore into the long swells of the Atlantic. Be careful of boat traffic as you pass the entrance to the harbor. The breakwaters do a very good job of hiding you from anyone operating a boat, so you may not be seen until you are in the harbor entrance.

The coast south of the harbor has a few small beaches but nothing like Crescent Beach, and cliffs soon rise almost directly out of the water. The cliff bases are strewn with boulders that look as if they had been dropped by huge dump trucks over the edge a hundred feet (30 m) above. There is nowhere to land here, and even getting too close to shore can be dangerous because of the confused waves patterns generated by waves being reflected back from the cliff in many directions.

Paddling a few hundred yards offshore will give you a new perspective on the size and composition of Block Island. The towering cliffs here are a slice through the glacial moraine that is responsible for Block Island's existence. Laid down about 12,000 years ago by the retreating glaciers, this huge moraine, which created Long Island, Block Island, Martha's Vineyard, Nantucket and Cape Cod, is slowly being eaten away by the pounding surf. As you pass around the southeast corner of the island you will see South East Lighthouse, a red brick lighthouse high on the cliff.

Originally built far back from the edge of the cliff erosion, it had to be moved when the cliff face had eroded to within a few yards of the building. A huge effort was mounted to save it. The entire building was jacked up and rolled back 270 feet (82 m) to its present location where it is now a major hiking and biking destination on Block Island. It also works as a great reference point for kayakers paddling around the island. When you pass the lighthouse you will be heading west and are about one quarter of the way around to the channel opening into Great Salt Pond. The last time I paddled around the southern end of the island there was virtually no wind, but the huge swells rolling in off the Atlantic precluded any attempt to land until I was just south of the channel into Great Salt Pond. Long gentle swells explode into white foaming fury when they reach the base of the cliffs.

The next navigational reference point along this shore is a large black rock, appropriately called Black Rock, that marks the southernmost point of Block Island. It is sometimes possible to get a bit of a break from large waves and swells behind this rock, which is only a few hundred feet offshore. If there is a strong wind, or the waves are coming out of Long Island from the west, it is very dangerous to get in among the smaller rocks surrounding Black Rock, so use caution paddling close to this boulder.

From Black Rock the coast curves gently north in a large arc, and the height of the coastal cliffs starts to drop. From South West Point to the entrance to the channel, the shoreline is punctuated by gravel beaches that get sandier the farther north you paddle. They make wonderful lunch stops. With the bluffs behind you and the ocean stretching away in front of you, these beaches are as solitary as you are likely to get on Block Island. Some of them are also reachable by hiking trails, so there is no a guarantee that you will have them to yourself. But in the spring and fall, it is very likely that you will only have a few boats and the smudge of land on the horizon that is Long Island to remind you of the outside world.

Sandy Point is home to the North Light, which began protecting mariners here in 1867 and is now a maritime museum.

North of Grace's Point — about two miles (3 km) up the western shore — the beach becomes more accessible from land, and the top of the bluff is dotted with cottages. The beach also becomes much sandier and the water much shallower. The inshore water is sprinkled with distinctively colored buoys that mark lobster traps, and further offshore it is dotted with sport fishing boats. There are a few rocky shoals here, so if you are paddling a composite boat, take care in this area. The breakwater sheltering the entrance to Great Salt Pond is marked by a light, and there are generally a few fishermen lining the water's edge.

The western shore, from the channel north to Sandy Point, is one long sand and gravel beach broken up by a few rocky areas. Thousands of nesting gulls live on this beach, particularly at the northern end. Please do not disturb their nesting areas, particularly in the spring. Gulls can be quite protective of their breeding grounds, and will swoop and dive at any intruder, including you. With a west wind making this shore less sheltered than Crescent Beach on the east side, there is no safe place to land on this entire stretch. But in an east wind it can be quite calm.

I prefer to enter Great Salt Pond here rather than continuing up the coast. For much of the year, paddling through Great Salt Pond is much like visiting a boat show by kayak. As one of the yachting destinations on the New England coast there are always dozens of beautiful boats moored in the harbor as well as boats leaving and arriving. Big boats tend gather in the southern half of the pond because the water is deeper there than in the northern part. When you paddle through the channel into the harbor you will be heading southeast. From here you have two options of which direction to paddle.

Your decision will be based partly on the tide. If the water level is high enough, it is possible to paddle into Trim's Pond. Its entrance is almost straight ahead when you come through the channel into Great Salt Pond. This will take you through the thickest concentration of boats but will put you on very sheltered water. From Trim's Pond you can paddle into Harbor Pond. The eastern shore of Harbor Pond is just a short distance from the ocean over some dunes. As mentioned earlier, it is possible to take your kayak out near the bridge and, using the road and a short path through the dunes, to portage directly onto Crescent Beach in a couple of minutes. You will come out less than a half mile (1 km) north of where you put in at the start of this circular paddle.

When you enter Great Salt Pond through the channel, another option is to head a little more easterly and aim for a small public beach that you will be able to see close to where Corn Neck Road, the main north-south road, is visible from the water. A wooden walkway will take you out to the road, and just a couple of hundred feet north is a cut through the dunes that will take you out onto Crescent Beach. I prefer the second option because it keeps you further away from the powerboats that frequent the southern part of Great Salt Pond. Launching from this beach through the surf can be exhilarating and a lot of fun. In the summer months there are generally a few surfers playing in the waves out here. If you want a calmer launch, head south through the two smaller ponds, but if you want fewer boats at the expense of a surf launch, take the more northerly route.

On very windy or rainy days, the three saltwater ponds, Great Salt Pond, Trim's Pond and Harbor Pond, can provide hours of exploration. At the far northern end of Great Salt Pond is a marshy area filled with bird life and few boats. Skipper's Island is also located up here and has some wonderful sheltered paddling around it. The Old Breach, which was cut through Harbor Neck into Great Salt Pond in 1889, is located just south of Skipper's Island and provides an easy landing spot from which to walk over to the western shore. In the spring nesting season this area is off limits for landing, but it is still a great paddling destination on windy days.

Along the eastern shore of Block Island, it is an easy there-and-back-again daytrip to the northern tip. It is possible to round the northern tip and paddle back down to Great Salt Pond and then portage back to Crescent Beach, but the hazard of paddling around the rips off Sandy Point at the northern tip makes this a paddle only for the very experienced. A better alternative is to paddle up the coast to Cow Cove, land and explore the North lighthouse and then return the same way. From

Great Salt Pond provides sheltered paddling on the windiest of days.

the northern end of Crescent Beach to Cow Cove, the shore is lined by tall, crumbly bluffs and has very few landing spots. There are a number of spots in which rocky shoals extend out into the ocean and the swells kick up huge explosions of spray even on calm days. The waves are positively spectacular here on rough days, with water shooting up almost as high as the bluffs. Of course you don't want to be out on the water when the waves are like that.

For days when you don't want to paddle or can't because of weather, Block Island offers many miles of hiking and cycling trails, several of which follow the coast and give views of the waves crashing on the beach and the rocks. Before European settlement, Block Island was heavily forested, but it now has large windswept moors with scrubby trees lining stone fences. There is a certain desolate beauty to this landscape. The Greenway Trails, created by the local conservation groups, make up a network of interconnected trails that cover the island. Some areas accessible from the trails include the South East lighthouse, the Mohegan Bluffs on which that lighthouse sits, dozens of freshwater ponds, Rodman's Hollow — a glacial ravine with an network of paths — and the Sachem Pond Wildlife Refuge, as well as the entire shoreline of Block Island. Much of the shore is very rugged and not fit for hiking, but it is all public.

Other off-the-water activities are shopping (not a lot, though) and just wandering around the small village. A seasonal theater presents movies at Champlin's Marina, and several hotels have live music in the evenings in the summer months. From Labor Day until Memorial Day, fall, winter, and spring, Block Island is very sleepy — the kind of place in which your best off-the-water activity would be reading a good book. The Book Nook of Block Island, an excellent bookstore in the village, offers a wide selection of books from works by local authors to the latest mystery. And the local library issues temporary cards to allow visitors to borrow books and check their e-mail.

While on Block Island I stayed at the Blue Dory Inn, a delightful little dollhouse Victorian inn just steps from the beach. From my room on the third floor I could look out over the water, and the sound of waves lulled me to sleep at night. The rooms are furnished individually in antiques and each has its own name as well as its own character. The staff seem like family and welcome you at the inn as if you were guests arriving in their home.

The Blue Dory Inn is part of a network of inns on the island called Victorian Inns by the Sea. Listed as one of the most romantic inns in New England — and the best place to be kissed in New England — the Blue Dory Inn is a wonderful place to go even if you don't paddle. But for paddlers it is doubly wonderful. There is an outside shower to rinse off your paddling gear and it is less than a hundred feet (30 m) to the water. The traditional continental breakfast is supplemented by daily specials and delicious omelettes, waffles, and pancakes.

I always made sure that I was back at the inn in the afternoon around teatime when their wine and very, very delicious cookies were available in the main parlor. This was a great time to meet the other guests to talk over the day's experiences and plan the next day's paddle. I am allergic to nuts, and the famous Blue Dory Inn cookies have walnuts in them along with huge chunks of chocolate. When I mentioned to another guest how much I wished I could have some of the cookies, one of the staff overheard me. The next day there was a special basket with my name on it full of Blue Dory Inn cookies with no nuts. Small wonder that this inn and the staff there secured a special place in my heart!

The Blue Dory Inn is a short five-minute walk from the ferry, an easy distance to carry, or better yet wheel, your kayak. As with most of the destinations in this book, a kayak cart that will fit in your boat is a wonderful addition — almost a necessity if you have to carry your gear and your kayak at the same time.

Rental kayaks and bicycles are available on the island close to the inn, but if you have your own boat this is an excellent destination to bring it to. Although it is possible to paddle over to Block Island from the mainland, I do not recommend it because of the distance, boat traffic, and changeable weather. This means you must either take a ferry over or fly. Time and budget are your main considerations as well as your decision whether to bring your own kayak or not. If you bring your own you will have to take the ferry. It is possible to rent kayaks at the places listed below. Many of them also rent bicycles, which means all you really have to bring to Block Island is yourself and your paddling clothes. Ferries leave from the following three ports: Point Judith, Rhode Island; New London, Connecticut; and Montauk, New York.

Block Island

INN INFO
The Blue Dory Inn ★ ★ ★ ★
P.O. Box 488, Dodge Street
Block Island, RI 02807
401-466-5891
1-800-992-7290
www.thebluedoryinn.com

MAPS & CHARTS
Waterproof Charts, # 2E
(large-print chart)

KAYAK RENTALS
Champlin's Kayak and Paddle Boat Rentals
P.O. Box J
401-466-7777
1-800-762-4541

Oceans and Ponds
The Orvis Store
P.O. Box 136
401-466-5131
1-800-678-4701

Payne's New Harbor Kayak Rentals
P.O. Box 112
401-466-5572

TRAVEL INFO

FERRY
From Point Judith and New London:
Block Island Ferry Information
Interstate Navigation,
401-783-4613
Cars are carried by reservation only. Call for schedule information.

From Montauk Point, NY:
Block Island Ferry Information
Viking Ferry Lines, 516-668-5700

Block Island, continued

Plane

Block Island has an airport that can handle private and commuter-sized aircraft. Scheduled service from Westerly, RI is offered by New England Airlines, and air charter service to Block Island is offered by the following charter airlines:

Resort Air
P.O. Box 577
1-800-683-9330, 401-466-2000

Block Island Airlines
1-800-411-3592

Maritime Airways
1-888-229-4449

New England Airlines
Westerly State Airport
Westerly, RI
401-596-2460

Quonset Airways
Block Island, RI
401-466-8900

Shoreline Aviation
New Haven, CT
1-800-468-8639

Train

Take **Amtrak**, 1-800-USA-RAIL, to New London to connect with the New London ferry to Westerly to connect with the Westerly Airport, or to Kingston to connect with the Point Judith ferry. From the Kingston Station, you will have to take a taxi to the ferry, about a 20-minute ride. The Long Island Railroad, 718-217-LIRR, connects to the Montauk ferry.

Bus

Rhode Island Public Transit Authority, 1-800-244-0444, operates buses to the Point Judith ferry.

Newport: Opulence, Tranquility, and Challenging Paddling

Newport is a city with a long history of the sea and of hospitality. Brass pineapple door-knockers on the front doors of many B&Bs around the world have become a symbol for the bed-and-breakfast industry, and this tradition started here in Newport. When a sea captain returned from a voyage, he would hang a pineapple on his front door to let his neighbors know that they were welcome to come and visit. So the pineapple was adopted by small inns and B&Bs as a symbol of hospitality. The afternoon tea was the favorite time for visiting, and this tradition continues to this day in Newport.

Newport inns and B&Bs set the standard by which all others are measured, and those featured here set a standard for those in Newport. It would be possible to paddle all of the areas described here from any of the three inns featured, but each inn nicely complements the paddling in the area with which it is matched.

Newport very neatly divides into three sections. To the east and south are the mansions on Bellevue Avenue and the Cliff Walk; to the north of the bridge to Goat Island is the older Colonial section, called the Historical Point area, which is filled with beautifully restored homes. Central to it all is downtown Newport, which focuses on Thames Street and the harbor. The paddling in each of these areas is distinct, and each holds its own fascination.

Newport is known worldwide as a yachting mecca. The Americas Cup race was run out of Newport for many years, and this harbor is the home of several 12-meter racing sloops. These graceful greyhounds of the waves are best seen from the water, and I know of no better way to appreciate their sleek lines than from a kayak. Boats of every size and description fill the harbor from Memorial Day until fall, making for some challenging navigation especially around the boating channels. Nevertheless, for a boat lover this is an area not to be missed. How often have you wandered along the waterfront and asked yourself what that boat moored out from shore looked like close up? Although it is strictly bad taste, not to mention illegal, to board a boat without permission from the owner, the water is public and

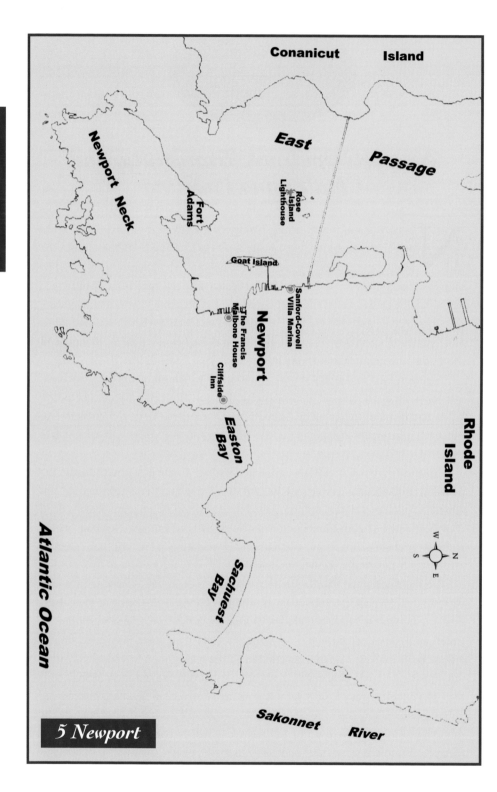

Conanicut Island

East Passage

Newport Neck

Fort Adams

Rose Island Lighthouse

Goat Island

Sanford-Covell Villa Marina

Newport

The Francis Malbone House

Cliffside Inn

Easton Bay

Rhode Island

Sachuest Bay

Atlantic Ocean

Sakonnet River

5 Newport

so it is possible to paddle through the flotillas of sailboats that grace Newport Harbor from May till October.

Of all the inns close to downtown Newport, the Francis Malbone House is the cream of the crop. It is located on Thames Street in the heart of the shops and restaurants of downtown Newport. The elegant three-story brick Colonial mansion has been restored and expanded since the 1970s. The discreet sign is the only indication that the large soft yellow building set slightly back from the road is an inn.

Once you are through the huge blue door a sense of serenity and peace envelopes you. It doesn't seem to matter how hectic Thames Street is; the door holds all thought of stress and noise at bay. The large guest parking lot behind the building gives easy access to the inn. Leaving your kayak on your car here is no problem; and it will be ready to go when you are. The inn is made up of two main buildings that are connected by a third around a garden courtyard. The sound of water splashing in the fountain can be heard in all the garden-side rooms.

The main building was built in 1760 as a private residence for Colonel Francis Malbone, a wealthy shipping merchant. In Colonel Malbone's day, Newport was one of the busiest commercial harbors in the new world. Now it may very well be one of the busiest recreational harbors in North America. In the restoration of the inn, secret passages were found leading to the wharf where the Malbone merchant ships would dock. Apparently much of the colonel's fortune was obtained by bypassing the customs agents of the King.

The inn was opened to the public in 1989 and was expanded in 1996 to double the number of rooms to eighteen. Its king-sized beds, jacuzzi baths, and attentive staff make staying at the Francis Malbone House Inn a true pleasure. Perhaps the most difficult part of your visit will be forcing yourself to get up and out on the water early enough to avoid the regular afternoon winds. In addition to the buffet of breakfast foods offered, the cooks at the Francis Malbone House Inn offer a hot specialty each morning, ranging from stuffed French toast to light fluffy waffles or delectable omelettes. There is only one hot entree offered each morning but what is lacking in variety is more than made up for in taste and there is a wide range of choices offered on the continental breakfast bar. Once you finish a decadent breakfast it is time to head out on the water.

There is a public launch ramp close to the inn, but the best place to put your kayak in the water is on the beach to the south of the harbor. Take Thames Street south and follow the signs to Fort Adams. Before you get to the fort, you will find yourself driving along with the harbor on your right. There are are two excellent launching spots, one on either side of a monument commemorating the landing of a French army to support the fledgling new country during the American

Rosecliff, one of the beautiful mansions on Bellevue Avenue in Newport, is just a short walk along the Cliff Walk from the Cliffside Inn.

Revolution. Park your car, unload the kayak, and prepare to paddle by some of the most beautiful racing and cruising yachts in the world.

The biggest challenge in paddling Newport Harbor is keeping away from the boat traffic and the main boating channels. In the summer months, especially on weekends, crossing the main boat channel can feel like trying to walk across a major highway. In a kayak you are not nearly as visible as most of the boats out here, but you can also go places that they cannot. Coasting along the shoreline and then in among the moored boats is the best way to paddle the harbor.

I tend to go up the outside first and over to Goat Island so that on my return paddle I can take my time among the yachts and get a good close look at the antique wooden boats moored along the waterfront. The hulls on some of these boats are so smooth and gleaming that I could see my reflection in them. Paddling along I would look up at the mast of the 12-meter boat beside me soaring into the sky, and the slight bend in the mast appeared to be an optical illusion. Then I paddled further away and realized that these boats have no straight lines. Everything has a slight, delicate curve that makes the boat appear to be constantly in motion even when it is resting lightly by the dock. Like Thoroughbred horses, these racing boats seem alive and ready to spring into action at a moment's notice.

If you time your paddle right, you will get to see these sleek craft sailing in and out of the harbor. Arrangements can be made to take a sail on some of the 12-meter boats as a tourist, and these cruises generally leave the harbor in pairs. This gives the illusion that they are racing with each other — a truly spectacular sight, whether they are competing or not.

Typically the winds on the harbor strengthen in early afternoon and can become quite strong in the late afternoon. This is your cue to head back to the inn, change into dry clothes, and have some afternoon tea. Freshly baked cakes and cookies along with cheese and crackers and fruit — and of course, tea — will curb your appetite long enough for you to browse through the listing of restaurants and plan your evening. If you feel you need to clean the salt off your boat and paddling gear, ask one of the staff and they will run a hose out to the parking lot so that you can rinse them off.

From this downtown location all manner of evening entertainments are within walking distance. Or you may chose to stay in and soak in your whirlpool tub to ease the paddling muscles and get them ready for another day on the water.

Newport calls itself "America's First Resort." Whether or not this is accurate, in the Victorian era it was certainly *the* place to be. A number of the wealthy elite built huge mansions along the coast overlooking the sea. Others built smaller castles and mansions in the same area, creating a neighborhood of elegance and wealth. Most of these places were summer homes used only a few months a year. Now you can visit some of the mansions and their gardens in public tours offered by the Preservation Society of Newport County, and get a glimpse of another era. It is also possible to arrange private visits to some of the mansions that are not open to the public. Yes, people do live in those places!

Along the edge of the bluff overlooking the ocean is the 3.8-mile (6 km) Cliff Walk. With the ocean on one side and the mansions on the other, this is truly a spectacular walk. But an even more spectacular way to see the mansions in all their grandeur is from the water, paddling along the shoreline in your kayak. From the waterline, the true proportions of the mansions become evident, as the size and layout of the grounds are clearer from a distance.

The Cliffside Inn is located just one block from the Cliff Walk, very close to Easton's Beach, which is the ideal put-in spot for this area. At the Cliffside Inn you will be truly pampered with wonderful breakfasts, opulent baths, accommodating staff, and very comfortable beds. Just staying at the Cliffside is a great vacation in itself, but staying there and then having such great paddling almost at the front door makes this a superb soft paddling destination.

Make sure that you fit your paddling into the time after breakfast on the verandah and before afternoon tea. The tea here is truly an event not to be missed, at least not by those of us with a taste for fine food and fine tea. The Cliffside has a table piled with delectable morsels ranging from stuffed pastries and fruit to rich, decadent desserts. In fact, the only difficulty with the tea at the Cliffside is stopping yourself from eating so much that you have no room left for dinner.

Rose Island Lighthouse is a perfect spot to stop for lunch, but make sure your kayak is pulled up well above the high-tide mark.

When you are ready for the day's paddle, head down the hill to Easton's Beach and get your kayaks wet. Parking can be a problem here in the summer, so if there are two of you, one of you may want to shuttle the car back to the Cliffside. It is only a five-minute walk away. It is possible to wheel your kayaks down to the water if you have a kayak cart, but getting them back up the hill to the Cliffside will take a bit more effort. From the soft sand of the beach the shoreline immediately rears up in a rocky wall with the Cliff Walk perched on top of it.

Time your paddle to be either at slack tide or just before low tide. If you paddle out just before low tide, you will have the current with you on the way out, it will be slack when you are at the furthest (and roughest) point out, and it will push you back in on the return trip. The tide does not run quite as strongly on this side of Newport as it does in the harbor entrance but there is still quite a strong current.

Be sure also to check the wind direction before you head out. With a strong northeast or north wind, it will be quite sheltered on the beach but will get progressively rougher as you paddle south alongside the Cliff Walk. A northeast wind here generally means bad weather as well, so if you are faced with a northeast wind it might be better to paddle around the harbor or up to the navy shipyard. With good weather, a favorable tide, and a wonderful breakfast under your belt, this is perhaps one of the most spectacular paddles in the Newport area. The rugged cliff undulates southward with the Cliff Walk outlining the crest. Behind the Cliff Walk, the estate grounds of the immense mansions slope up to their grand stone facades.

With a light swell, the rolling water explodes in huge geysers of spray at the base of the cliff. Much of the cliff is undercut, and in several spots there is evidence of man's puny attempts to hold back the destructive power of the sea. The further south you paddle along the shore, the rougher the shoreline gets. Eventually, close to the Breakers — one of the largest mansions — there are a couple of offshore islands that break up the force of the ocean and have allowed a small bay to form. There is even a small beach here at low tide just below the Oriental teahouse on the Breakers estate.

After the teahouse is behind you, the cliff becomes much lower and the shoreline more broken up. The coast has been slowly sweeping around to the west and you are now exposed to the full power of the ocean. As I was paddling through the many rocky islets here one reasonably calm day, a rogue wave that had been funneled and compressed between some islands slapped me right over. One second I was paddling along with an annoying but small following sea, and the next second a 5-foot-high wall of water hit me broadside almost at right angles to the regular wave direction. I fortunately was able to snap right back up and there were no other strange wave patterns to bother me, but it could have been a cold swim.

The water out here in spring (it was early May at the time) is quite cold, and this incident brought home to me the dangers of paddling in these waters in larger waves or bad weather. On my return to Easton's Beach, I headed far enough out from the rocks to minimize any chance of being hit by any waves that were reflected or compressed by the rocks. When I headed out further from shore, the true scale and proportions of the individual mansions on the top of this bluff becomes even more apparent. What I found amazing was that some of the larger mansions visible from the water were not among those that are open to the public; they are actually private homes that modern-day Vanderbilts live in.

Another wonderful spot to paddle that is just a short drive from the Cliffside Inn is the Sakonnet River, in and around the bird sanctuary. This area is best accessed by kayak from the public beach a couple of miles (3 km) east of Easton's Beach. From here you can paddle around the point and up into the Sakonnet River. Make this a full daytrip and take a picnic lunch with you. As you paddle along the shores here, keep clear of the fishing lines that the surf fishermen have out. It is very hard to see them sometimes, but if there is a fellow standing out in the surf there is likely a line or two angling out into the water.

As you paddle here you will see many different species of birds, especially during spring and fall migration times. It is in fact far easier to see the birds and other natural phenomena here from a kayak than from the land. The land is covered in very dense foliage, which makes the paths in the reserve feel like green tunnels or canyons. The variety of seabirds here is especially diverse.

Returning from a long paddle to high tea at the Cliffside Inn is one of the true pleasures of this soft paddling destination. While nibbling on delicious hors d'oeuvres and sipping fine tea, I met a friendly couple from New York who were on their seventh visit to the Cliffside Inn. That seemed amazing to me until I started asking other guests if they had been here before and found that over half the people I talked to were return guests. Many of them come just to get pampered at the Cliffside Inn. The fact that they were in Newport seemed to be secondary.

All of the people I met here seemed to be friendly and relaxed. It is just not the sort of place that people come to for business. In fact, a couple of the folks I talked to seemed a little put off when they saw me with a laptop computer. Once I explained that I was not checking stocks or keeping in touch with the office but was writing a book, they immediately relaxed. Afternoon tea on the porch can draw out to several hours of conversation often followed by an invitation to join one another later for dinner.

The third area of Newport is located north of the Goat Island connector bridge. Entering this district — the Historic Point district — transports you back to a previous century, with restored Colonial homes, working gaslights on the small narrow

A rare calm day on the south shore of Newport offers the option of paddling in the wide-open Atlantic.

streets, and a complete absence of commercial advertising. There are many delightful small inns and B&Bs in this area, but only one is directly on the water. The Sanford-Covell Villa Marina Bed and Breakfast has a long name that reflects a long history. It was built in 1869–70 as a summer cottage for a New Yorker, M.H. Sanford, according to a design by William Ralph Emerson, a cousin of Ralph Waldo Emerson. This was before the huge mansions on Bellevue Avenue, Rhode Island's most famous street, and it is thought to have inspired some of the construction there.

The three-story tall entrance hall with balconies protruding at different levels and stairs sweeping up one wall set the tone for the rest of the house. The current owner, a descendant of William Covell, who purchased the property in 1895, has been slowly restoring the building to its former grandeur. Although not as elegant as the Cliffside Inn or the Francis Malbone House, the Sanford-Covell Villa Marina feels like a comfortable, even opulent, family cottage where the guests are given the personal attention of the owner and the small staff. The two large pianos in the front parlor are available for guests to play. While I was there, a couple looking for a room came in and played the pianos for quite some time.

As a soft paddling destination, the location of the Sanford Covell Villa Marina is hard to match. It has its own private dock and, better still for kayakers, there is a public boat ramp right alongside the villa. The ramp is not used much except by locals and so is an excellent launching site. Straight out from the ramp is Rose Island, crowned by the Rose Island lighthouse. To the north is Coasters Harbor Island, the site of the Naval War College and Museum. North of that are US Navy ships, which are open to the public to tour. Touring around an aircraft carrier in a kayak is a real exercise in proportion and perspective.

My favorite paddle from here, though, is out to and around Rose Island. Much of the island above the high tide line is off limits to people in order to protect the sensitive habitat of the birds that nest here. It is possible to land and explore the lighthouse and area immediately adjacent to it. Rose Island Light Station was abandoned by the Coast Guard in 1971 and the years between 1971 and 1984 saw the buildings fall into neglect and be damaged by vandalism. In 1984 the non-profit Rose Island Lighthouse Foundation was formed to preserve and operate the lighthouse as a historic and environmental site.

The light is now maintained by folks who pay for a week-long stay and the chance to act as lighthouse keepers. If you are interested, you might want to call right away. The family on duty when I visited had waited three years to get there. It seems that being a lighthouse keeper for a week is very popular. It is also possible to stay overnight in the summer months, but once again the wait list is extremely long.

Rose Island is completely self-sufficient. All fresh water used is collected from rainwater and all electricity is wind-powered. It is a delightful place. The lighthouse has been restored to its 1912 condition, and work continues to restore other areas and maintain the light. In the spring and fall, field trips from area schools come out and enliven the island with shouts of discovery. The island is closed to the public before 10 A.M. and after 4 P.M. Please respect the privacy of those who are living here for the week and leave them in peace.

When paddling out to Rose Island, take into account the tidal currents. They can be very strong especially on the western side of the island. The tides go up and down quite rapidly in this area, so make sure when you land that your kayak is above the high-tide mark or at least out of danger of an incoming tide. The bastion on which the lighthouse is perched is a perfect spot for lunch and boat-watching. All types of vessels, from small day-sailers to large tall ships and huge ocean liners, pass by this point. One day when I was there, a large ocean liner had anchored outside Newport harbor and the local sailing school was using it as an island to sail around. The flotilla of tiny sails emphasized the huge size of the ship they were sailing around.

The only problem I had with boat traffic in this area was with a couple of yahoos on personal watercraft. They were not expecting a kayak, and cut very close to me on both sides. I don't think that it was intentional but if they had hit me, the effect would have been the same, intentional or not. Be very careful out here. There is a lot of water traffic, and in a kayak you are not very visible.

Paddling north to the Naval War College will take you under the toll bridge and away from much of the Newport boat traffic. Some boats do sail out of this part of the harbor, but not nearly as many as from further south. And the shoreline is not as interesting as in other areas around Newport. But rounding that last point and seeing huge gray warships moored in front of you is quite an experience.

Make sure that you return to the B&B in time to sip some sherry or port while basking in the sunset. The porch here is a perfect spot to watch the day disappear in a blaze of color and talk over where to go for dinner.

As Newport is a tourist destination, it offers many rainy-day and off-the-water activities. First and foremost would be a tour of the mansions. The Preservation Society of Newport County has restored and preserved eight homes as museums. These luxurious, opulent mansions concentrated around Bellevue Avenue offer a glimpse into the gilded age of Newport when it was the summer home of the wealthy, from southern plantation owners escaping the southern summer heat to the early industrialists building "cottages" for summer use. One can easily spend a couple of days wandering through these gorgeous estates.

Newport has always had close links with the sea and boatbuilding, and the International Yacht Restoration School located right downtown on Thames Street continues that tradition. The school rebuilds and preserves old ships and yachts in need of a home. If you are a boat lover, this school is a must to visit. Traditional and modern boatbuilding methods are used to restore yachts to their former glory. And as I mentioned earlier, it is possible to arrange an excursion on the old Americas Cup boats to get a feel for what these sleek yachts feel like under sail. There is a naval museum to the north of town that allows you to tour several warships, and for those more interested in navy history it is possible to visit the Naval War College.

The drive around Ocean Drive to Brenton Point State Park then back along Bellevue Avenue will give you a good overview of the area. And of course, it is well worth taking the time to walk along the Cliff Walk and see on land some of the same areas you have paddled by on the water. Fort Adams State Park is the site of historic Fort Adams as well as the Museum of Yachting, both of which are well worth a visit. Finally, as can be expected, there are numerous antique shops and galleries in town.

INN INFO

Cliffside Inn ★ ★ ★ ★ ★
2 Seaview Avenue
Newport, RI 02840
1-800-845-1811
401-847-1811

The Francis Malbone House
★ ★ ★ ★ ★
392 Thames Street
Newport, RI 02840
401-846-0392
1-800-846-0392

Sanford-Covell Villa Marina
★ ★ ★
72 Washington Street
Newport, RI 02840
401-847-0206

MAPS

NOAA # 13221 at 1:46,500

RENTAL OUTFITTERS

There is currently no rental outlet in Newport that rents cockpit sea kayaks and also allows you to transport the kayaks on your own car. It is therefore advisable to rent a kayak close to your home if you are driving or to bring your own if you own one. It is possible to rent sit-on-top kayaks here but using one limits your paddling destinations.

The Kayak Centre
888-SEA-KAYAK
Wickford Store (main store)
401-295-4400
Newport Store 401-848-2920

TRAVEL INFO

Newport is accessible by car, train, bus, and air.
Having your own car will allow you to access more remote paddling but it is possible to paddle in Newport without a car.

Wellfleet: Tides and Terns

The alarm woke me from a sound sleep and I lay in bed staring at the ceiling trying to figure out why I had set the alarm to go off so early. Then it hit me — the tide would be high slack in two hours. We had just enough time to get up, have breakfast, and get on the water an hour before high tide so we could paddle out of Drummer Cove at slack tide and ride the ebb tide out to Great Island. Paddling on the Cape Cod Bay side of Cape Cod requires a close watch on the tides. The further south in the bay you travel the higher the tides are. Here around Wellfleet the tidal range can be over 9 feet.

When we had turned in the night before, the area in front of our B&B was a sea of grass with glistening patches of black mud showing through in long ribbons. These ribbons of mud marked the deepest parts of Drummer Cove directly in front of Drummer Cove Bed and Breakfast. And now, standing on the balcony overlooking the cove in the morning, we could see the water lapping at the shore just a few feet from where our kayaks were drawn up on the salt grass. We had a quick breakfast with our hosts, Ruth and Reuben, threw on our paddling gear, and launched the boats. It would be ten hours before the water would be high enough for us to return comfortably to this spot. We had packed a picnic lunch and some other snacks and were planning to spend the entire day exploring Wellfleet Harbor.

Wellfleet Harbor almost divides Cape Cod in two. It is just under a mile (2 km) overland between the tidal flats in Drummer Cove and the Atlantic shore. Many lobster boats and other fishing craft moor in Wellfleet Harbor. In addition to these working boats you will see dozens of pleasure craft and small rowboats moored at buoys set out from the shoreline. An hour's paddling west from Drummer Cove will bring you out into the deeper water of the harbor proper. Watch along the shoreline in this stretch for horseback riders. They can often be seen cantering along the edge of the tidal flats. Look down in the water and you will see cultivated oysters riding on long lines running into the depths. Oysters and other shellfish are a big part of the local economy and are strictly controlled by fishery officers.

Before you start, take your bearings. To the south is Lieutenant's Island and to the north is Indian Neck; straight ahead across 2 miles (4 km) of open water is Great Island. As you head north along the beaches of Indian Neck, you will see many different manmade attempts to halt the process of erosion, all of them unsuccessful. Huge gigantic concrete blocks stacked against the bluff are tossed aside like so many children's blocks. Long breakwaters made of huge jumbled stones angled out from the shore are slowly being sucked down into the sand. In some places the entire bluff behind the beach is encased in a sheathing of stone and concrete, but large sections have slipped away, leaving gaping holes from which sand dribbles down in a slow steady stream. This is a locale in which waterfront property is very expensive and desirable but not very permanent.

Indian Neck Beach, the public beach at the north end of Indian Neck, has a long jetty jutting out into the harbor. Behind the jetty and breakwater, large fishing vessels lie at anchor in a tight group, or are tied to the wharf. The edge of the group of big fishing vessels marks the edge of the dredged channel and anchorage in the inner harbor. At low tide the decks of some of these boats are at the same level as the surrounding tidal mud flats.

You can stop at the wharf in Wellfleet for a cup of coffee or a lobster dinner. The only problem is finding a place to park your kayak while you eat. If you don't want to spend the entire day on the water, you could leave your vehicle here at the main wharf or near Mayo Beach, where there is free public parking and beach access.

Continuing on past the beaches of Wellfleet, it is best to stay a little distance offshore so as to avoid any swimmers. You will likely see some windsurfers whizzing across the bay water, as they generally land and launch on this next stretch of coast. The northern end of Great Island is quite close now, just across a channel leading to Herring River.

The Herring River is a very short stretch of water that runs under the road at a causeway bridge and leads into a very swampy area. Birdwatchers will love the Herring River, especially in the spring and fall when thousands of migrating waterfowl move through this area. If you ride the ebb tide current out of the mouth of the Herring River and back into Wellfleet Harbor, be careful to clear the shoal off the point of Great Island. Even in a kayak it is possible to get hung up here at low tide.

We planned to have lunch along the shore of Great Island below the south facing bluffs. It was late October and we were looking for a sheltered spot to catch some sun. We ran our kayaks up on the shore about 100 feet (30 m) from the high tide line, and dragged them further up so we could tie them up to a large boulder. Sitting on a log on the beach eating lunch in the sun, it was hard to believe that it was closer to Hallowe'en than it was to Labor Day. We stripped down to shorts and T-shirts and soaked up the sun while we worked our way through a huge lunch.

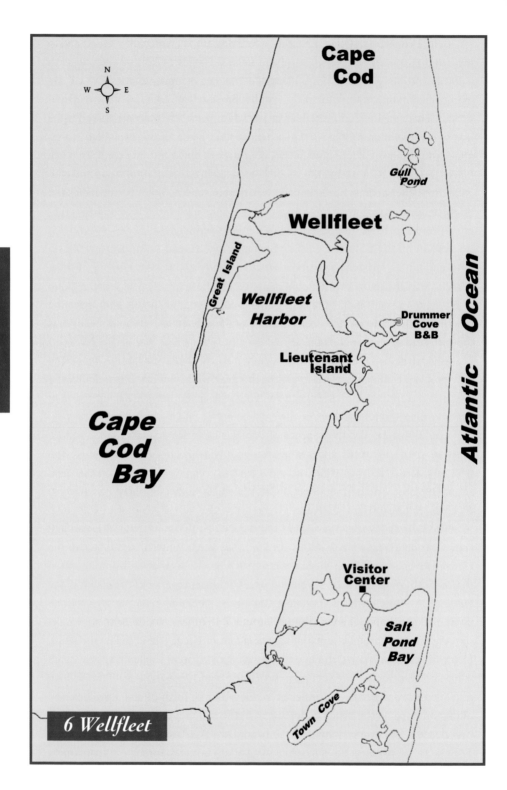

Cape
Cod

Gull
Pond

Wellfleet

Great Island

Wellfleet
Harbor

Drummer
Cove
B&B

Lieutenant
Island

Cape
Cod
Bay

Visitor
Center

Salt
Pond
Bay

Atlantic Ocean

Town Cove

6 Wellfleet

The ability to paddle comfortably this late in the year is one of the great advantages of soft paddling.

After lunch the sun nearly lulled us to sleep, but we wanted to get to the tip of Great Island and Jeremy Point before we headed back to Drummer Cove. By then the kayaks were about 300 feet (100 m) from the water but the tide was starting to flow in again. By the time we had everything loaded up and were back in our paddling gear, the water had crept another 50 feet (15 m) closer. We dragged our boats to the water and had to continue dragging them for some distance because the water was still too shallow to float a kayak. Once on the water we headed south along the shore of Great Island.

The eastern shore of Great Island is made up of two long, high bluffs, one facing south and the other at an angle facing east. Between these two bluffs is a narrow sandy pass that leads over to the Cape Cod Bay side of the island. The large marshy area here between the bluffs shelters many different types of ducks and gulls as well as a few herons. Further south, the bluffs dwindle into dunes and finally into expansive sand flats. The shoreline here is always changing, with wind and waves shaping and moving the sand. Amazingly, there are a few clumps of grass at the highest point of this sandy world. This is Jeremy Point. It's hard to believe that under these sands and some of the dunes on Great Island there was once a village. Very little of this settlement remains to be seen on Great Island, and nothing of it is left on Jeremy Point.

I got out to walk over to the Cape Cod Bay side to see how rough the water was and to decide whether to paddle around the point into the open bay. What seemed like a short walk from the kayak took me fifteen minutes to cover on the hard flat sand. When I reached the dunes I turned to look for the kayak and it seemed very far away with a long line of footprints trailing off into a blurred line before they reached the kayak. The waves from the open waters of Cape Cod Bay were crashing on shore with a violence that seemed unbelievable compared to the calm on the Wellfleet Harbor side of Jeremy Point.

Just off the southern end of Jeremy Point is Billingsgate Shoal, a very shallow tidal flat that is normally covered by water except at the lowest tides. The water above this shoal and for some distance around it becomes very turbulent with tidal races running over the shoal and compressing up into steep waves. This is an area to avoid in any type of boat, but especially in a kayak on an ebb tide. If you were to dump in this area on an ebb tide you would quickly be swept out into Cape Cod Bay.

Your return route to Drummer Cove will depend largely on the weather conditions. In moderate weather it is a straight 2 miles (3 km) to the tip of Lieutenant Island from Jeremy Point, and the only hazard in this crossing is boat traffic. If the weather is unsettled, it is far wiser to paddle north to cross over to Indian Neck,

Provincetown offers colorful buildings, great galleries and lots of shopping.

where you will be more sheltered and have less open water to cross. Make sure you time your arrival to slack high tide. We missed the tide once and were stuck hauling our kayaks through knee-deep stinking mud. No matter how you arrive, be sure to rinse down your boat and body before you head inside for your long hot shower.

The tall glass front of the Drummer Cove Bed and Breakfast will draw you in from your paddling like a beacon guiding a sailor home. No matter what room you have in the house, they all have a balcony and an ocean view. From your private balcony you can look out over the water you just paddled or you can join Ruth, Reuben and the other guests on the deck or in front of the towering fireplace inside. There are few other buildings close to the Drummer Cove B&B, so it is possible to get a clear view of the stars. On a clear night they're like bright lights sprinkled across the sky.

An option for a nice half-day trip from Drummer Cove B&B is the paddle south along the Cape Cod Bay shore around Lieutenant Island. The south shore of Lieutenant Island is a Massachusetts Audubon Society Sanctuary, as is the mainland shoreline across from the south shore of the island. Landing here is not allowed, but it is a wonderful place to view wildlife, especially birds. You will notice on your paddle through the channel between Lieutenant Island and the mainland that the road is much lower than the bridge. If you paddle through here at high tide — which is quite likely, since you have to leave Drummer Cove about an hour and a half before high tide to have enough water depth to go out and return in a four-hour period — you may be able to paddle right over the road.

At the highest tides, the island is cut off from the mainland until the water begins to drop again. The large tidal flats south of the island surrounded by marsh provide an ideal bird habitat. It is also possible to visit this sanctuary by road. There is a wonderful interpretive center that is in itself worth the price of admission, and an extensive network of trails and boardwalks that allow you to get close to the marsh habitat. We returned from here as the sun was setting over a stained-glass sea, silhouetting small boats riding at their moorings — a picturesque way to end a soft paddling vacation.

Two other paddling destinations easily accessed from Wellfleet require that you drive to put-in points. The first is just a couple of miles (3 km) away and gives you a chance to paddle on calm freshwater ponds. Gull Pond is a large glacially formed kettle joined to a series of other smaller water-filled kettles just to the north. Kettle ponds are formed when a huge piece of ice buried in the debris left behind by a retreating glacier melts. As the huge ball of ice melts, the land caves in around it creating a circular hole in the ground. Wherever these holes are deep enough to tap into the underlying water table, they form kettle ponds or lakes. Gull Pond is one of these. On the western shore of Gull Pond just off Gull Pond Road there is a public launch area. In the summer and on some fall weekends these ponds can be very busy, but for the rest of the year they are a wonderful quiet retreat. It only takes a couple of hours to completely explore them, but on a windy day or if you just want a break from salt-water paddling, they are a calm, shady destination.

The second paddling destination close to Wellfleet is Salt Pond, Salt Pond Bay and the connecting waterways. Salt Pond can be seen just outside the Salt Pond Visitor Center of Cape Cod National Seashore. Just off Route 6, the visitor center is full of interesting and informative displays about the natural features of Cape Cod. A few hundred feet (100 m) south on Route 6 is a steep driveway leading down to a town launch ramp. Leaving your car here but is not permitted, but you can unload and then return your car to the large parking lot at the visitor center.

Salt Pond is an almost completely round pool with a narrow outlet leading out into the much larger Salt Pond Bay. Salt Pond Bay in turn connects to Nauset Bay to the north and Nauset Harbor to the south. If you paddle south through Hemingway's Channel, a windy channel that is closest to the mainland, you will end up in Town Cove. Town Cove is also connected to Nauset Harbor and is the ocean access for Orleans. Incidentally, Goose Hummock, the best kayak rental place on Cape Cod, is located on the waterfront on Orleans just off Route 6A.

The paddling options and areas to explore from Salt Pond include everything from facing the raw power of the open ocean (for the very experienced) to endless wandering through the channels in the salt marsh grass. At high tide, the entire area is one big waterway with a few small low islands scattered around. At low tide, the area turns into a giant maze of waterways running in every direction. The only area that might cause problems for inexperienced paddlers is the entrance to Nauset Harbor. If you are caught here on an strong ebb tide, you risk being swept out into the Atlantic and having to deal with the large waves and crashing surf along this shore. If you do paddle through this area, make sure that that it is at slack tide or on an incoming tide. This way there is no danger of being swept out through the channel into the open ocean.

It is possible to paddle down from Salt Pond and go for lunch in Orleans. There are several places to eat close to the water, and the folks at Goose Hummock can recommend somewhere to you. If you have rented boats from Goose Hummock, then you may want to turn the route around and paddle up to the Salt Pond Visitor Center. About halfway between Orleans and Salt Pond is Fort Hill. There is a short hiking trail around this hill and up to the lookout at the top. The view from the top is well worth the hike, since it allows you to look out over the entire area you have paddled and will be paddling. Be sure to secure your kayak if you plan on stopping here or in Orleans. Even if you are renting a boat, it is a good idea to bring a long cable lock with you on your trip to Cape Cod, to prevent unauthorized users from trying out your kayak when you are not in it.

The last time we paddled this bay, there was a strong wind that created small waves on Salt Pond Bay and made paddling a bit challenging but not at all difficult. Looking out over the barrier dunes on Coast Guard Beach, we could see spray blowing up to 30 feet (10 m) in the air. There was a constant line of foaming white visible over the barrier dunes. When we returned to our car we headed over to Coast Guard Beach, and were astonished to find that the onshore wind was so strong we could hardly stand up. Some local surfers shivering on the beach after doing battle with the waves told us that it was the best and biggest surf they had ever seen there. I was very glad we weren't out in those waves in sea kayaks!

If the weather turns so bad that you can't paddle or if you just want a day off the water, Cape Cod has many, many options for things to do. Visit Provincetown and tour the galleries and wander through the colorful streets. Climb the tower in Provincetown built to commemorate the landing of the Pilgrims here in 1620. The Pilgrims didn't stay; they moved across Cape Cod Bay to Plymouth a month after they landed, but this was where they first set foot in the New World. The Italian-style Pilgrim Monument gives you a 360-degree view of Cape Cod. From here you can clearly see how the shifting sands have shaped this land.

The Cape Cod National Seashore has a good exhibit building at the northern end of the Cape. You can visit the site of the first radio tower at the Marconi Station Site, or you could pay your respects at the John F. Kennedy memorial in Hyannis. If you like bicycling, Cape Cod has a network of paved bike paths running the length of the peninsula. It is a great way to work out some non-paddling muscles, and in some cases you can ride close to the same routes you have paddled. Ruth, the hostess at Drummer Cove B&B, is a fount of information about hiking possibilities in the area. Of course you can also just stay at the B&B, read, and watch the sun set in a crimson blaze of color as you relax on your balcony.

Wellfleet

INN INFO

Drummer Cove Bed and Breakfast ★ ★ ★
1100 Blackfish Lane
Wellfleet, MA 02663
508-349-1127
Off-season 201-261-2032
www.anm.com/lees/drummer

LOCAL INFORMATION

Wellfleet Chamber of Commerce
P.O. Box 571
Wellfleet, MA 02667
508-349-2510
www.capecod.net/wellfleetcc
wellfleet@capecod.net

TIDES

www.maineharbors.com
The B&B also has information on tides.

MAPS AND CHARTS

Cape Cod National Seashore
Published by National Geographic, waterproof and tearproof, perfect for kayaking. Available at the Cape Cod National Seashore visitors center.

RENTALS

The Goose Hummock Shop Original Store
Route 6A, P.O. Box 57
Orleans, MA 02653
508-255-0455

The Goose Hummock Shop Outdoor Center
(kayak rentals)
On Town Cove, Box 57
Orleans, MA 02653
508-255-2620
www.goose.com
goose@capecod.net

TRAVEL INFO

Cape Cod is a drive-to destination. There is very little public transit available. Bring your car but plan on cycling and paddling as much as possible.

Chatham: Elegance and Dunes

Cape Cod from the air looks like a bent arm extending out from the mainland. At the elbow of that arm, in the south eastern corner of Cape Cod is the small community of Chatham. Just off the eastern shore of the coast here is a long string of constantly shifting barrier islands. Behind these islands lie sheltered bays filled with bird and marine life that couldn't have been better designed as great paddling spots. On the outside of the barrier islands are large waves and surf and enough challenging paddling to satisfy any hard-core surf and open ocean paddler. On the inside of these islands is calm sheltered water and miles of gentle paddling.

Chatham Bars Inn is the best inn for soft paddlers to stay at in this area. One of the world's best small inns, the Chatham Bars Inn is a perfect base from which to paddle this area. With their own private beach to launch from and access to both inner bay and outer ocean from this beach, it would be hard to find a better place from which to explore this area. The Inn also offers an excellent children's program and they actively encourage their guests to bring their children with them.

Chatham Bars Inn was built in 1914 to plans by Boston architect Harvey Bailey Alden. Originally the Inn focussed on hunting as the main activity but hunting is no longer part of the activities available at the Inn. Golf, tennis, archery swimming and, of course, paddling are now the activities practised by the guests of the Inn as well as just relaxing on the porch in the wicker furniture sipping a cocktail while you gaze out over the ocean. Or if you prefer somewhere a little more private, take your cocktail to the gazebo where the ocean views are just as wonderful but the setting is far more intimate. The main dining room has one of the best ocean views of any dining spot in New England. Seated at a table by the huge windows overlooking the southern end of Pleasant Bay and the surf crashing into the dunes beyond is a perfect place to plan your next days paddle or retrace the route you just paddled. The formal elegance of dining here is a wonderful juxtaposition with a day spent paddling in the waters visible through the windows. In addition to the main inn building there are numerous cottages with suites and individual rooms in them. Some of these cottages are right by the beach and others are set back from the water near the golf course. In the 205 rooms here, there is something that will suit almost everyone. The shingled buildings, expansive ocean views, impeccable service and elegance of the Chatham Bars Inn will take you back to a more slow-paced and civilized era.

A huge buffet breakfast is served each morning in the dining room overlooking the ocean. From your table by the window you will be able to see the many different colors of water running in undulating bands across the bay. The deepest water is the darkest, a dark blue gray on sunny days, and this is where the big fishing boats moor. The water graduates in ever lighter bands, each lighter tone indicating a slightly shallower area. On a calm day it is possible to chart out a morning paddle from the windows of the dining room by following the mid-toned blue water up the bay. Remember where those patterns lead when you get out on the water paddling.

The most obvious paddling spot here is straight off the beach and up into Pleasant Bay. Pleasant Bay extends north along the Atlantic shore of Cape Cod, sheltered from the open ocean by the barrier dunes. In places this barrier is quite tenuous, and periodically in huge storms breaches will be made in the barrier dunes by the pounding surf. These breaches come and go with the passing years, and the whole barrier dunes and islands area moves around so much that charts are only good for a few months after they are printed. The most recent major breach was created in 1987 almost directly across from Chatham Bars Inn. This small breach grew with each passing storm, and now the once-sheltered shoreline of Chatham village is exposed to the full fury of winter gales.

We don't need to worry about the shifting dunes in a kayak but we do need to worry about the tides here. Not only are the tidal currents quite strong but the bay is quite shallow and it is possible to get stranded on the wrong side of immense sand bars. The hotel has a tide chart posted in the front lobby along with a weekly events schedule. Make a note of high tide times and plan on paddling around that time. You will have a good two hours on either side of high tide in which you will have no worry about being stranded. It is best to leave the Inn's beach on a flood tide so that you can ride the current up into the bay. Then after slack tide you can ride the ebb flow back to the Inn. Pleasant Bay offers many different types of paddling due to the large area covered by the bay. Bounding the eastern edge of the bay are the barrier dunes, which hold back the full fury of the ocean.

As Heather and I paddled close beside the dunes we could hear the crash of the surf on the far side of the dunes and the spray from the waves crashing down was clearly visible over the dunes. It was a nasty windy November day but the paddling inside the dunes on Pleasant Bay was quite pleasant. We pulled up our

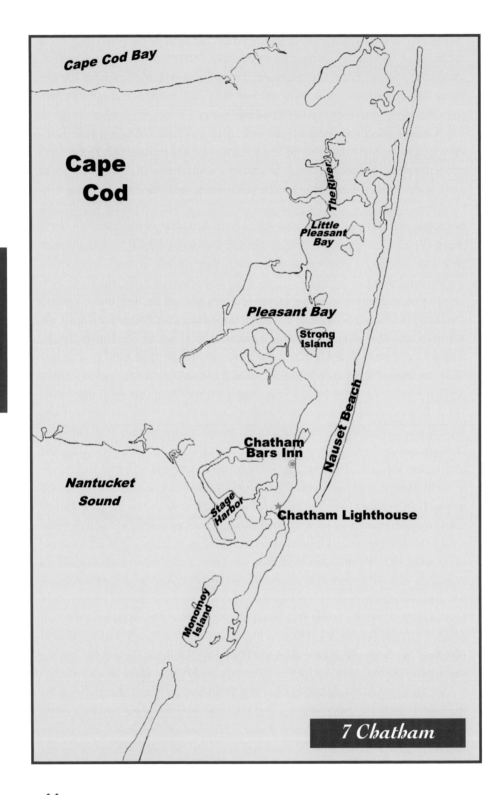

Cape Cod Bay

Cape Cod

The River

Little Pleasant Bay

Pleasant Bay

Strong Island

Nauset Beach

Chatham Bars Inn

Nantucket Sound

Stage Harbor

Chatham Lighthouse

Monomoy Island

7 Chatham

kayaks at a spot where a beach road came close to the water and walked across the dunes to look at the surf. A line of 4x4 trucks, with and without campers attached, were parked on the beach rocking in the wind. The owners of these rigs were surf fishermen scattered along the shore in ones and two like so much human flotsam. The waves crashing in on the beach that November morning were at least 10 to 12 feet high yet on the Pleasant Bay side of the dunes there were only 5-to-6-inch ripples. Wandering back to our kayaks we noticed dozens of huge horseshoe crab shells scattered among the sea grass. Some of these shells were over a foot across. Inside one shell we found a tiny crab no bigger than the end of my thumb.

If you take the time to look for it, you'll find a huge variety of marine life hidden in this bay. In the spring and fall there is an influx of migrating birds that fill the sky in flocks, gaggles and flights. Just down the shore from the Chatham lighthouse, we saw a migrating hawk hovering in the wind. For several minutes he stayed in one spot, just moving the very tips of his wings to keep in position. Further up the bay several groups of cormorants were forming up for the flight south. These birds, so ungainly in the air and on take-off, must be doing something right since they have hardly changed in millions of years of evolution. Many types of gulls were circling around the different islands defending their territory with raucous calls.

Gulls are not unintelligent birds despite the fact that they seem to fight needlessly among themselves. I saw one gull fly up into the wind with something in its beak. The bird maneuvered itself over a pile of rocks on the shore and dropped what it was carrying in its beak from about 30 feet up. There was a loud crack when the object hit the rocks, and I paddled closer to get a better look. The gull, totally uninterested in me, swept down to the object and immediately flew back up with the same object in his beak. I was close enough now that I could see that it was a clam or mussel shell that the gull was carrying. Once the gull had reached the same spot again it flew a bit higher and again dropped the shell on the rocks. Another loud crack and the shell was broken. The gull settled down to a feast of mussels on the half shell and I paddled away thinking about the mental process required to think that maneuver up. I left with a growing appreciation for the abilities of a simple gull.

Chatham Harbor turns into Pleasant Bay just north of Strong Island. Be careful of the large tidal flat extending out from the southern shore of Strong Island. If you keep to the channel about halfway between the barrier dunes and Strong Island you should have no worries about grounding here. Soon after you pass Strong Island you will see the salt marsh grass of Sipson Island poking above the water. The tidal flats extending out from this almost submerged island are even more extensive than those around Strong Island. Once you have threaded your way through the channels leading through the flats you will enter Little Pleasant

Looking northeast from Chatham Bars Inn, you can see both Pleasant Bay and the open Atlantic.

Bay. The further north you paddle, the bodies of water on which you paddle get consistently smaller and more protected. A side benefit to this is that there are fewer and fewer motorboats the further north you paddle because the water is just too shallow for most of them.

Sampson Island forms the eastern boundary of Little Pleasant Bay. At low tide Sampson Island is connected to the barrier dunes by hard-packed sand flats. Make sure you paddle around Samson Island on the western side unless you want to get in some practice portaging kayaks.

North of Little Pleasant Bay the water divides into two channels around Barley Neck. The eastern channel winds up between Barley Neck on the west and Pochet Island on the east. Pochet Island is tied to the barrier dunes by a marshy area and this channel soon peters out in a narrow shallow marshy creek. Paddling up through this channel will take you into wonderful birdwatching territory. Just make sure you keep a good watch on the tide as well to ensure you don't get stranded up some little marshy channel.

The western channel heading east around Barley Neck is called the River. The River has three narrow leads running into several kettle ponds. These narrow twisting waterways are much like rivers except they flow in different directions depending on the tide. You are guaranteed sheltered paddling in these small waterways. These waterways have names such as Namequiot River, which leads to Areys Pond, Meeting House Pond, Keseayo Gansett Pond and, my favorite, Frostfish Cove.

Little Pleasant Bay is separated from Pleasant Bay by the Sipson Islands. You passed Sipson Meadow rising just above the water on your way north, but the other two islands carrying this name rise further from the water. The deepest channel runs in between the wooded shores of Sipson Island and the mainland. The point running out to meet Sipson Island has a hole in the end, known as the Horseshoe because of the shape of the shoreline. Named the Narrows, this channel can have very strong tidal currents running through it, as water drains out of Little Pleasant Bay on an ebb tide. The Sipson Islands and Strong Island to the south make up the central islands of Pleasant Bay.

From the central islands of Pleasant Bay you can head to the western shoreline and follow it south through the convoluted coves and bays that make up the many small harbors on this coast. There are dozens of traditional cat sailboats in these small harbors along with other more modern craft. The catboats with their mast stepped far forward in the bow and the traditional gaff-rigged mainsail have changed little over the last hundred years. These are very graceful craft, gliding over the water like huge birds with wings spread out to catch the wind. If you are a wooden boat lover you will likely spent a lot of time paddling in among these beautiful old boats. The return route down the eastern shore of the bay takes you

Much of Pleasant Bay's tidal flats disappear below water at high tide but are the perfect place for a long walk at low tide.

by many large mansions and smaller quaint cottages as well as through several harbors filled with commercial fishing boats. Eventually you will see the Inn beckoning to you across the water and your pace will pick up as you think of a nice hot bath followed by cocktails on the porch. Pull your kayaks up on the beach above the high water mark, rinse off in the outdoor showers by the pool, and then head to your room to get ready for an evening of refinement.

The paddling options heading south from the Chatham Bars Inn entail one of two things. Either you are comfortable paddling in very treacherous water seething with riptides and huge waves or you will have to make a short portage across the sands of Chatham Beach. Twenty years ago, before the breach in the Nauset Beach barrier dunes, it was possible to paddle in sheltered water past the lighthouse around the corner and into Stage Harbor. Since the breach in the dunes and subsequent shifting of the shoreline, the southern barrier dunes have joined with the mainland and bar access to the south. The width of this sand barrier changes from year to year but it is generally only a short haul taking no more than a few minutes to transport your kayak from the open channel leading out into the Atlantic to the sheltered water behind what used to be the bottom end of Nauset Beach. Stretching south from Cape Cod like a tattered scarf, the Monomoy Islands divide Nantucket Sound from the Atlantic Ocean. North Monomoy is sheltered from the full strength of the Atlantic waves by the barrier dunes of Chatham/Nauset Beach. It is likely you will not be bothered by many motorboats around North Monomy Island, as the water over large areas is only a little over a foot in depth. This shallow water, especially on the west side of the island, can turn a short paddle into a long walk if you get caught by low tide.

Birdwatching on the Monomoy Islands is very popular especially around spring and fall migration times. Other wildlife you may see in the area are seals, but they tend to be far more common in the late fall and winter. South Monomoy Island does not benefit from any protection and is only fit for very experienced paddlers. The heavy surf dumping on the eastern shore extends all the way around the tip and offers no real escape routes in case of trouble. Unless you are an accomplished surf paddler, stay around North Island and spend any extra time exploring Stage Harbor. From Stage Harbor you can paddle into the Oyster Pond River, which leads to Oyster Pond or into the Mitchell River, which will take you into Mill Pond in the heart of Chatham Village.

There are several excellent restaurants in Chatham in addition to the three at Chatham Bars Inn. The inn keeps a binder in the lobby with all of the local restaurant's menus in it so you can make a decision on where to eat before you leave. On a rainy or very windy day the village of Chatham offers great shopping — window and real — as well as several excellent galleries.

If the weather turns so bad that you can't paddle or if you just want a day off the water, Cape Cod has many options of things to do. Visit Provincetown and tour the galleries and wander through the colorful streets filled with very colorful people. Climb the tower in Provincetown built to commemorate the landing of the Pilgrims here in 1620. The Pilgrims didn't stay, they moved across Cape Cod Bay to Plymouth a month after they landed but this was where they first landed in the New World. Pilgrim Monument gives you a 360-degree view of the shifting sands of Cape Cod. The Cape Cod National Seashore has a good exhibit building at the northern end of the Cape, you can visit the site of the first radio tower at the Marconi Station Site or you could visit the John F. Kennedy memorial in Hyannis. The rest of Cape Cod is minutes away by car and there are many bike trails through out Cape Cod. If you are a cyclist as well as a paddler you will definitely want to bring your bike on any trip to Cape Cod. The inn has bikes for rent if you don't bring your own. The network of bicycle trails on Cape Cod crisscrosses the land like a net. You can travel almost anywhere by bike on a bike path, and once off the bike path, the roads are smooth and safe to bicycle as long as you stay off the main arteries.

Chatham

MASSACHUSETTS

INN INFO
Chatham Bars Inn ★ ★ ★ ★ ★
297 Shore Road
Chatham, MA 02633
508-945-0096
1-800-527-4484

OTHER LOCAL INFO
Chatham Chamber of Commerce
29 Village Landing
Chatham, MA 02633
1-800-945-1233

TIDE INFO
There is a tide chart in the inn lobby.

MAPS AND CHARTS
Cape Cod National Seashore
Published by National Geographic, waterproof and tearproof, perfect for kayaking. Available at the Cape Cod National Seashore visitors center.

RENTALS
The Goose Hummock Shop Original Store
Route 6A, Box 57
Orleans, MA 02653
508-255-0455

The Goose Hummock Shop Outdoor Center
(kayak rentals)
On Town Cove, P.O. Box 57
Orleans, MA 02653
508-255-2620
www.goose.com
goose@capecod.net

TRAVEL INFO
Cape Cod is a destination you will have to drive to. There is very little public transit available.

Plymouth: Pilgrims and Paddling

Plymouth holds a unique place in American history. The image of the Pilgrims with their big black hats sitting down to the first Thanksgiving feast is firmly entrenched in American folklore. The Pilgrims did bring the custom of a harvest feast with them from England, and indubitably they were very thankful for having a harvest to celebrate after their first summer here. But the Pilgrims arrived in Plymouth only in early December in 1620 and had to survive their first winter, with the help of the local Natives, on supplies they had brought with them from England. The local inhabitants were the Wampanoag, and some of their descendants still live in the Plymouth area. Without the help of these people, the Pilgrims would not have survived and flourished, and we would not now have the great Thanksgiving holiday.

The paddling in the Plymouth area covers much more than just Plymouth Harbor and environs. The coast of Cape Cod Bay bends south in a long gentle curve from Plymouth Harbor to the entrance to the canal through the neck of Cape Cod. There are hidden little harbors along the coast that offer sheltered bird-watching. The waters of the open bay can be dangerous in high winds and will offer enough of a challenge to the most experienced kayaker. Paddling around Plymouth Harbor will take you back in history and also give you a chance to check out a wide variety of boats from the waterline. Inland, there are freshwater ponds, some of which are joined by narrow streams just barely deep and wide enough to be navigable by kayak. With the large variety of paddling options, you had best plan to spend a few days in this area.

It is possible to stay right in Plymouth, but if you did, you would have to drive to every launch point. I found it much better to stay a few miles south of Plymouth on the shores of Cape Cod Bay. There are three B&Bs located on or near the shore, all of which are excellent bases from which to explore the paddling options in the surrounding area. Each of the three B&Bs featured here has its own particular style. Stay at whichever one suits you best.

A short 6.5 miles (10.5 km) south of Historic Plymouth, and Plymouth Rock

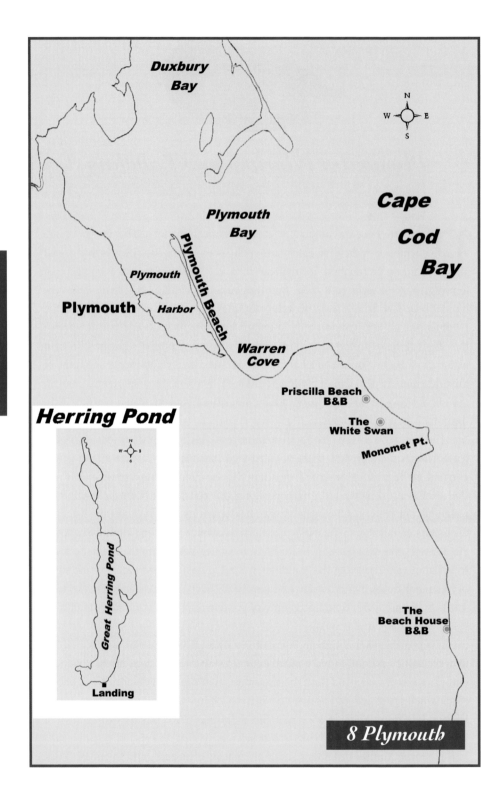

Duxbury
Bay

Cape

Cod

Bay

Plymouth
Bay

Plymouth

Plymouth

Plymouth Beach

Harbor

Warren
Cove

Priscilla Beach
B&B

The
White Swan

Monomet Pt.

Herring Pond

Great Herring Pond

Landing

The
Beach House
B&B

MASSACHUSETTS

8 Plymouth

is the Priscilla Beach B&B. Built in 1865, this classic Victorian home is a delightful base for paddling in this area. Even driving up to the front of the B&B takes you back to another era because of the old 1930 Model A Ford (named Annabelle) sitting in the driveway. Meticulously renovated and restored by its owner in 1999, the Priscilla Beach Bed and Breakfast is an elegant and relaxing place to rest.

At low tide, Priscilla Beach (actually the north part of White Horse Beach) stretches as wide as a football field, its flat, hard sand ending in gently curling breakers. Launching at low tide requires a long walk across the sand, and almost always means launching through surf. If there is an east wind or a storm brewing, don't even think about launching here. On calmer days and with a high tide, Priscilla Beach presents a completely different face — calm, gentle and very inviting. If you are staying at the Priscilla Beach B&B, it is a short 500-foot (150 m) walk to the water. If you have wheels for your kayak, this is an easy trip, but if not it might be best if you drove down to the access point and unloaded your kayak there. Then you can return your car to the B&B or, if you are alone, ask Brian, the B&B's owner, to drive it back for you.

Your decision whether to paddle north or south should depend to a certain extent on the tides. You are not far down into Cape Cod Bay, but there is still a tidal fluctuation here that can generate currents that it's better to not paddle against. When we arrived at Priscilla Beach B&B, one of the first things Brian did after making sure we were settled in was to give us a local tide chart. Armed with this information, we decided to paddle north first; but when you paddle it may be better to paddle south first and ride the tide down into the bay. Whichever direction you paddle, remember that this is an out-and-back paddle, so you are only halfway there when you turn around. The trip back often seems longer when you are tired, even if you do have the tidal current helping you. Let's first cover the route north of the beach and then talk about the paddling options heading south from White Horse Beach.

The shoreline north of the beach climbs rapidly into a sandy bluff with a rough boulder beach running into the water. Several large boulders sprinkle the shoreline and offer shelter to migrating ducks and other waterfowl. We saw a Harlequin duck swimming along just out from these rocks as we paddled by. The long bluff running north along the water is broken at one point by a large industrial building on the shoreline — a nuclear power station. On the north side of the station is a breakwater sheltering what appears to be the mouth of a creek. It is in fact the outlet for the warmed-up water used to cool the reactor. When warm water meets cool water, marine life seems to proliferate, and there are always several fishermen trying their luck in this area. I am not sure if I would want to eat the fish living beside a nuclear power station, but the fishermen swear there is no danger.

A beautiful day on Priscilla Beach, an excellent place to practice surf landings and launchings.

A twenty-minute paddle north of the power station, the shoreline curves east at Rocky Point. This is a good area to spot seals in the fall. The shoreline is so steep and rugged here that almost all signs of civilization disappear for a while. If the water is calm enough, the huge rocks at the base of the bluff provide an excellent spot for a short picnic.

Continuing on past Rocky Point, heading east now, you will notice that the natural rocks slowly disappear to be replaced by man's feeble attempts to stop erosion. Perched along the top of the cliff are huge luxury homes that the sea is constantly trying to pull down into the water. The tall sandy bluffs are visibly crumbling — in some spots you will see tiny avalanches of sand running down the cliff face like dry rivers. After a heavy rain or northeasterly storm, huge chunks of the bluff peel off and crash on the shore below, sometimes taking expensive real estate with them. Paddling along beneath these bluffs, keeping a healthy distance away from them, I realized that we kayakers get the same view and solitude that these homeowners are looking for, but we don't have to worry about our kayak disappearing in the next big rainstorm.

Stretching out in front of you as you paddle along this shoreline is a long golden sand beach barring all access to the west. This beach forms the back of Warren Cove. Directly ahead, the beach backs on mainland and you can see the road into

Plymouth running along the shore behind a couple of hotels. These hotels are good spots to stop if you fancy lunch at a restaurant. North of the buildings, the beach becomes Plymouth Beach, the ocean side of a long sand spit sheltering Plymouth Harbor. There are a few buildings on this narrow spit of land, but most people come here to lie on the sand and play in the waves.

In the summer months the beach here will be very crowded during the day, but in the spring and fall you will likely have it all to yourself. I would not recommend paddling out to the end of the spit for a few reasons. It is a long way back to your put-in point, and that sand spit is longer than it looks. Also, the tidal currents and shallow bottom make paddling around the tip of Plymouth Beach very unpredictable and dangerous. Finally, there is a lot of boat traffic in and out of the entrance to Plymouth Harbor that can be quite hazardous to those in kayaks.

If you do leave Warren Cove and paddle along the edge of Plymouth Beach, be careful of getting caught in the steeply dumping surf. On warm summer days this would be a great area to practice surf landings and launchings, but the current regulations on landing a kayak on a public beach in this area are unclear. In the spring and fall there is no problem with beach access, but I would be wary about landing here in the summer. The tip of the sand spit is a protected nature reserve, and landing is not permitted.

When you return to Priscilla Beach you will be faced with two options. You can land or you can continue down past where Priscilla Beach blends into White Horse Beach, and paddle out around Manomet Point. This high bluff was the site of a life-saving station. The rails on which the lifeboats ran down the steep shore into the water are still there but they have been bent and twisted by the fury of winter storms. The stories of the dedicated and intrepid lifeboat men who risked their lives to save others are quite inspiring. Offshore from these tall cliffs are several rocks that create a tricky paddling area and a refuge for wildlife and marine life. Once you are past the blocky shape of Manomet Point, the shoreline becomes gentler for a while and is lined with cottages and homes on a private beach. (The coast south of here is covered in the next section of this chapter.)

Halfway between the nub of Manomet Point and the entrance to the Cape Cod Canal is a small bump on the shoreline of Cape Cod Bay called Center Hill Point. Just a short way along the shoreline bluffs from this point, you will find a delightful small B&B perched high on the bluff, with a steep path leading up through the boulders from the water's edge to a deck overlooking the water. The Beach House B&B offers a wonderful view over Cape Cod Bay from this deck where breakfast is served if the weather is warm enough. Sipping tea after breakfast, comfortably ensconced in a chaise lounge on the deck watching the mist burn off the water on an early fall day, you might find it hard to motivate yourself to actually get off the deck and into your kayaks.

It is possible to carry your kayaks down the path to the water from the little lawn between the deck and the edge of the bluff, but a far easier put-in can be found just a short way back down the road you drove in on. Ask Denise (the hostess at the Beach House B&B) to arrange temporary access to the water's edge for you through their neighbors' lane. If you do decide to launch from in front of Beach House, plan your launch for a mid-tidal range period. With a high tide, the waves crashing directly onto the rocks make landing a very tricky business; and at lowest tide it is very difficult to pick your way out through the rocks to the short breakwaters running out from the shore. At mid-tide the breakwaters shelter a small strip of sand from which it is easy to launch, and then you can thread your way out through the rocks guarding the entrance.

Once away from land, take some time to look back at the shoreline you have just left and memorize what the shoreline looks like in this spot. It can be very hard to distinguish exactly where to land on your return if you have not memorized the shoreline. If in doubt, place a flag or tie a bright jacket or sweater to the rocks or handrail to make it easier to identify the right place to land.

The shoreline north from here to Manomet Point looks much the same as it does right in front of the B&B, dropping here and there to shallow reedy beaches and then rising again to sandy bluffs shored up with hundreds of tons of protective rocks. The tops of the bluffs and the shoreline between them are dotted with homes and cottages of every imaginable size and vintage. It is possible to continue around Manomet Point to White Horse Beach and beyond. If you plan to do this, refer to the above description for details.

South of the Beach House Bed and Breakfast, the shoreline is lower, and if you follow it, you will eventually reach the entrance to Ellisville Harbor. Ellisville Harbor is not a big harbor; in fact, the entrance can be so shallow at some times that even a kayak will scrape the bottom. This area is a very delicate ecosystem with wonderful opportunities for birdwatching. As we drifted into the quiet waters of the lagoon, pushed on by the strong tidal current, we watched a pair of piping plovers scurry along the shoreline. The current of the incoming tide was strong enough to run my bow firmly onto a shoal in the middle of the channel. It felt like river paddling more than sea kayaking.

Further into the harbor we silently glided along channels in the salt grass following a pair of swans deeper into the marsh. After more than an hour spent exploring the many channels through the inland area of the marsh, we headed back out toward the harbor entrance again. We had dropped our car off here earlier because Heather wanted a shorter day of paddling and we had parked it far back from the water's edge. By now the water was lapping at the tires and we had to paddle right past the car to reach solid ground. I quickly jumped out of my kayak, gave Heather my bow line, hopped into the car, and drove it to even higher ground. By the time we had loaded Heather's kayak on the rack, the tide waters had already started to recede.

The tidal fluctuation increases the further south you get into Cape Cod Bay. Here, less than 15 miles (24 km) south of Plymouth as the crow flies, the tide rose and fell over a foot (30 cm) higher than in Plymouth. These differences are compounded when it is a full moon, which it would be the evening following our paddle. Riding the ebb tide, I was swept out through the harbor entrance and into large waves that developed while we were paddling in the harbor and marsh area.

South of Ellisville Harbor the shoreline becomes increasingly steep until it is a cliff running several miles south to Sagamore Beach. As for all beaches in Massachusetts, the regulations governing the landing and launching of kayaks on Sagamore Beach are seasonal and user-dependent. For the most part it is not a good idea to try to land between Memorial Day and Labor Day, but at all other times you will be safe landing here. A word of caution, though: when there is a high tide and a northeast wind, the steep waves make this beach extremely difficult to land on. On an ebb tide there is even a bit of an undertow, so be extremely careful if you plan on landing here.

The weather here can change quite quickly, especially in the fall. What had been a nice calm day with a gentle westerly breeze when we had launched at the Beach House B&B changed over a period of four hours into a cloudy day with strong winds from the northeast, and steep 4-to-5-foot (1.5–2 m) waves. The ebb-tide current running north under the gray seas that were marching south created very challenging paddling. I had a lot of fun plowing through the waves but I was very glad Heather was not with me. This is the type of paddling she hates — lots of work, cold water, and very slow headway. The same distance that had taken an hour to cover in a lazy paddle in the morning took two and a half hours of steady slogging to paddle with the change in the weather conditions.

Landing at the Beach House B&B would have been impossible if the tide had not been in the middle of its fluctuation. As it was, I was grateful to be paddling a plastic boat, as I bounced off a few rocks while threading my way into the narrow strip of sand. It took two of us to carry the kayak up to the safety of the lawn where we locked it to Heather's and tied it off to a stake. A quick shower warmed me up, and with raging appetites we headed out in search of dinner. There are several excellent restaurants in the area and your hosts will be able to direct you to one that suits your mood.

Paddling around the Mayflower *in Plymouth Harbor.*

The White Swan B&B is located in White Horse Beach just south of Priscilla Beach. The White Swan has been an inn and B&B continuously for decades. Although the operators might change, the place itself will always be a comfortable home at the end of a day exploring. Since this B&B was a bit further from a launching spot, and because the weather was not as calm as it had been when we were at Priscilla Beach or the Beach House, we decided to explore the more sheltered paddling options in the area.

First, we sat down to a huge breakfast with the other guests at the inn. Meeting other travelers like this is one of the best things about soft paddling in smaller inns and B&Bs. After breakfast we donned our paddling gear and drove out to the closest inland pond. These freshwater ponds dot the entire area and make a pleasant change from battling the saltwater power of the ocean.

Great Herring Pond is a long, shallow lake with an excellent public landing at the southern tip. Paddling north from the landing, you will see a large complex of building on the western shore about a third of the way up the lake. This is a sailing center, and watching the sailboats race around a triangle course with a few sailors tipping themselves and their boats right over into the water provides endless entertainment for a kayaker. The entire shoreline of this pond is forested and ringed with cottages and homes. Other than the put-in point, there is nowhere to land.

At the north end of the pond is the outlet of a creek that at first glance seems too fast, shallow, and narrow to accommodate kayaks. But if you push and pull your way up through the shallows, under the bridge, and through into the woods on the other side, you will find yourself on an exploration of another side of Massachusetts. Once the road is left behind there is very little indication of homes nearby or other infringements by mankind. You will paddle under low trees and through sun-dappled groves of aspen and birch. Birders will love this paddle, as forest birds rarely seen on ocean paddles flit through the trees around and above you.

At one point you will pass bridge abutments on either side of the creek. Watch for spikes in the wooden remnants of the bridge submerged in the water. Above the old bridge the creek widens and becomes more sluggish and windy. Along the shore in a few places here are cranberry bogs, and if you time your visit to coincide with the harvest you may notice the harvesters walking the fields with their motorized harvesters. Eventually you will come out through a marshy area into Little Herring Pond, which stretches north for another couple of miles (3 km).

The trip back down the creek is faster because you have the current with you, but you may find yourself wishing for a shorter, more maneuverable kayak in some sections. Be especially careful when you head out into the lake if the current is up. It is quite easy to flip here if you are not used to river paddling. Remember when crossing a current in a river to lean downstream, away from the waves. It seems backward to those who have always paddled on the ocean and have only dealt with waves on the ocean, but it does make a difference.

Another paddling destination in the area to which you must drive to find a put-in point is Plymouth Harbor. Plymouth Harbor is the location of what could be considered the most famous landing in the United States. The landing of the Pilgrims at Plymouth Rock is a strong image in American history. The rock now sits under a Greco-Roman pavilion at the edge of the water in Plymouth. It was moved to its current location in order to make room for a new dock, and was not always held in such respect as it is now. At one point there was even some question about which rock really was Plymouth Rock. All the controversy is laid to rest now, and the rock can be seen from shore-side.

A much better way to see the rock is to paddle up to the grating and see it from a rock's eye level just partially submerged in the waters of Plymouth Harbor. Plymouth Rock is a few minutes' paddle along the shore from the wharf where the *Mayflower* is moored. On weekends and in the summer there are always lots of people staring at this lump of granite, using it as a touchstone to connect with American history. From the waterside you will likely be on your own with all of the other tourists on the far side of the rock.

The best put-in for Plymouth Harbor is actually just north of the harbor break-wall. There is a small beach here close to a stream outlet, and as long as the wind is not too strong, this is a great place to launch from. It is also possible to put in right off the strip of grass and rocks bordering Water Street. Parking here can be a real challenge except in the spring and fall, but if there is a space it is possible to lower your kayak over the rock retaining-wall and paddle right off the main tourist street. The third put-in option is at the south end of the town, but there is some debate about the legality of kayaks on this beach during the summer months.

Dozens of active fishing boats, whale-watching boats, and what seem to be hundreds of pleasure craft, are moored in the actual harbor area. Sleek Alden-designed yachts are moored beside simple catboats and fiberglass weekenders. On summer weekends, this is a very dangerous place to paddle because of the high volume of boat traffic. But there are a couple of unique boats and shoreline features that make this paddle worth doing no matter what the traffic or weather. First and foremost of these is the *Mayflower*. This is a replica of the original *Mayflower*, moored at a wharf just a few minutes' paddle from Plymouth Rock.

One hundred and two people left England on September 6, 1620, aboard the *Mayflower*, and they first sighted land off the tip of Cape Cod three months later. Two of them died on the crossing, and one child was born before they reached land. These courageous settlers created a new society here in the New World that they hoped would be free from religious persecution. Many American traditions have come from the Pilgrims, Thanksgiving being the best known. Paddling along-side the *Mayflower* and looking up at the towering stern that tapers to a small platform high above the water, I was struck by the audacity of packing 102 people and animals into this small ship to sail across the Atlantic to a completely unknown world. The next time someone asks about the dangers of sea kayaking, I will have to remember to compare it to the dangers the Pilgrims faced. The current *Mayflower* is a beautiful reconstruction, and it is well worth taking the time to tour the interior from the dock, but you will have a much greater appreciation for the inside of the ship after you have paddled around it.

Paddling south from Plymouth Rock, you will pass a large yacht club, and then the shoreline becomes much less urban. The further south you paddle, the closer you get to the sandy dunes that back Plymouth Beach. At the bottom of the harbor all that separates you from the open water on Cape Cod Bay is the sand spit of Plymouth Beach. It is also possible to paddle north from the breakwater on the northern edge of the anchorage in front of downtown Plymouth. Straight north, the tower of Standish Monument marks the northern edge of the bay and the domain of the wealthy. Out toward the east, two lights mark the entrance channel to Duxbury Bay.

Looking at Plymouth Rock from the waterside. The Greco-Roman Pavilion shelters the rock from the weather.

Duxbury Bay is the northern portion of Plymouth Harbor. It is a sheltered body of water bounded by the Plymouth Beach sand spit on the southeast. Reaching down from the north to almost touch Plymouth Beach is the long sand barrier of Duxbury Beach. If you are an experienced paddler, it is possible to paddle out here. But be extremely careful around the channel entrance; the tidal currents are very strong here and can easily sweep you out into the open bay water. If they are combined with a strong west wind, they make this a very, very difficult place to paddle. It is not uncommon for waves to triple in size once you're beyond the shelter of the barrier sand spits. Be careful!

Plymouth and the surrounding area offer many off-the-water or rainy-day activities. The first of these would be the reconstructed Plimoth Plantation. This "living museum" gives an extremely accurate historical recreation of the life of the early Pilgrims, complete with actors and interpreters in period dress. Just to the north of downtown Plymouth, right on the waterfront, is the Ocean Spray cranberry museum, which is well worth a quick tour. To visit Boston, you could take a short drive north or take the train from Kingston, a few minutes north of Plymouth. Cape Cod is an easy daytrip from this area, and, of course, there is always the option of just relaxing at the B&B.

INN INFO

**Priscilla Beach Bed and
Breakfast ★ ★ ★**
7 Morse Rd.
Plymouth, MA 02360
508-224-7448
877-977-4222
http://members.aol.com/prisbeach
/index.html
E-mail: PrisBeach@aol.com

Beach House B&B ★ ★ ★
429 Center Hill Road
Plymouth, MA 02360
508-224-3517
1-888-262-2543
http://members.aol.com/prisbeach
/index.html
E-mail: PrisBeach@aol.com

The White Swan ★ ★ ★
146 Manomet Point Road
Plymouth, MA 02360
508-224-3759
Fax: 508-224-1948
1-888-713-7190
www.whiteswan.com
invasa@capecodinternet.com

MAPS AND CHARTS

NOAA Chart, Cape Cod Bay.
This is a very large-scale chart
and does not cover the inland
ponds. Check with the local
rental agencies for charts when
you rent.

RENTAL OUTFITTERS

There are no local outfitters but
the Goose Hummock Shop on
Cape Cod rents kayaks.

**The Goose Hummock Shop
Original Store**
Route 6A, Box 57
Orleans, MA 02653
508-255-0455

**The Goose Hummock Shop
Outdoor Center**
(kayak rentals)
On Town Cove, Box 57
Orleans, MA 02653
508-255-2620
www.goose.com
goose@capecod.net

TRAVEL INFO

This is a destination where you
need a car to fully explore the
paddling options in the area.
Boston is very close and is
accessible by plane, train and
bus. Cars can be rented at the
airport in Boston.

Cape Ann: Artists and the Atlantic

C
ape Ann is a gnarled nub of granite thrust into the Atlantic a short distance north of Boston. The two communities on Cape Ann, Gloucester and Rockport, are quite distinct from each other despite their proximity and shared history. Both towns have roots extending back to the late 1600s, and fishing was the mainstay of each town until quite recently. Gloucester is still an active fishing port with much of the waterfront on the harbor devoted to commercial fishing. It is a town with no pretensions, although it has become more upscale in the past few years. It has a rougher nature downtown than on Rocky Neck and Atlantic Avenue. The tourist accommodations are primarily on the outskirts of town, leaving the center of the city to commercial enterprise, museums, and public buildings. Gloucester has received a great deal of attention lately due to the central role the city plays in the book and movie *The Perfect Storm*.

Rockport, just a short paddle away near the tip of Cape Ann, is an artists' community filled with dozens of galleries, charming shops, and every other tourist service imaginable — except one. Rockport is a dry town. If you want to drink alcohol here you will have to bring it with you. The harbor at Rockport is divided up by high granite block walls into sections resembling huge rooms. Each section has a different type of boat in it. There is a section filled with lobster and fishing boats, one with larger sailboats, and an area with small sailing craft. There is a kayak rental place on the harbor in Rockport on Bearskin Neck. North Shore Kayak Outdoor Center offers guided tours, kayak rentals, kayak leasing, and retail sales. They are an invaluable paddling resource in this area.

Paddling Cape Ann can be done in several ways. It is possible to stay at a B&B in Gloucester, then paddle to a B&B or inn in Rockport, and then continue on around the Cape to return to the first B&B in Gloucester. I have done this route, and it gives the satisfaction of never backtracking and actually traveling by kayak. It does have its problems, though. It is completely weather- and skill-dependent. If the weather is bad or if your skill level is not up to paddling in the open ocean, then it is not safe or possible to do this route. The circumnavigation of Cape Ann

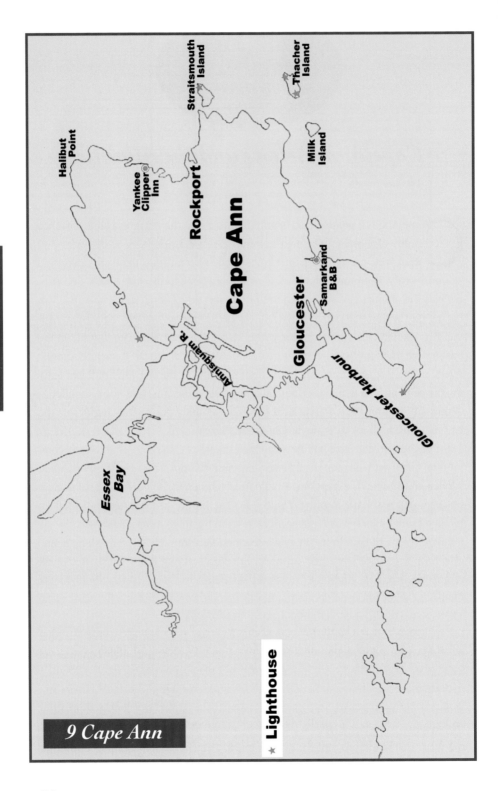

MASSACHUSETTS

9 Cape Ann

Halibut Point

Yankee Clipper Inn

Straitsmouth Island

Thacher Island

Milk Island

Rockport

Cape Ann

Gloucester

Samarkand B&B

Annisquam R.

Essex Bay

Gloucester Harbour

★ Lighthouse

also necessitates paddling through Gloucester Harbor, which is extremely busy and quite dangerous in a kayak. The Annasquam River, really a tidal estuary that cuts across the neck of Cape Ann, is also quite choked with powerboat traffic for most of the summer. The river can be quite a nice paddle mid-week but is best avoided on the weekends. The short canal that joins the river to Gloucester Harbor has a strong tidal current flowing through it that can be quite tricky to paddle in if you are not used to 10-knot currents.

Basing yourself in Rockport allows far more flexibility in route planning and doesn't depend on the appearance of the weather conditions needed for a complete Cape Ann circumnavigation. It is possible to do several trips out of Rockport Harbor, ranging in length from a couple of hours to a full day. The convolutions in the rocky coastline have produced a few small but excellently sheltered harbors. Beyond the harbor entrance, however, the shoreline varies from huge granite boulders and exposed bedrock to sandy beaches hidden at the backs of some of the coves.

There are three islands off the coast of Cape Ann, two with lighthouses and the third with thousands of birds. Thacher Island has two tall stone lighthouses that are visible for miles and make an excellent navigational reference point; Straitsmouth Island has one lighthouse on it that is visible from Rockport Harbor. Milk Island, the third island off the shores of Cape Ann, is home to thousands of birds. If you do paddle out here, do not disturb their nesting areas by landing on this island. It is their home; we are just here to look not land. There are also two large partially submerged rocky shelves called the Salvages, straight out into the Atlantic from Rockport Harbor, on which harbor seals can occasionally be seen basking. Another rough granite outcropping rears from the sea off Good Harbor Beach.

Compared to Gloucester, Rockport is very kayak friendly. There is a great kayak rental shop right on the harbor: the North Shore Kayak Outdoor Center. They also offer bike rentals and guided paddling daytrips in the area. If you stay in Rockport, it is not necessary to bring anything more than your paddling clothes and street clothes on a soft paddling adventure here. It is not even necessary to bring your car, since you can arrive by train directly from Boston. The folks at the Yankee Clipper Inn will pick you up at the train station.

The artists of Rockport have filled dozens of galleries along the narrow winding streets with works spanning the whole range of visual arts media. There is something here for every taste, from abstract art to photography to landscape painting. Bearskin Neck is a narrow point of land separating the old harbor from Rockport Harbor. This neck of land is crowded with shops offering everything from antiques to fudge and is a delightful place to wander around just people-watching and window-shopping. Most of Rockport is best seen on foot. Parking is generally not available in the center of the village, and in any case, most things are only minutes apart by foot. The roads on Cape Ann are smooth, scenic, and not too hilly, which makes them perfect for exploring by bicycle. If you are not planning to paddle every day of your trip here, bicycling is the next best way to explore Cape Ann.

Sitting in the Veranda restaurant at the Yankee Clipper Inn, I gazed out over the water while I waited for my breakfast to arrive. The water looked like a rumpled blue sheet dotted with dozens of colorful hard candies. Reds, yellows, blues, greens, pinks — every color of the rainbow — was sprinkled over the water. Each splash of color marked a buoy floating above a lobster trap. Every small-scale lobster fisherman has his own distinctively colored pattern for his buoys so he can easily find his own traps. These colorful floats are dotted around much of the Cape Ann coast.

I had paddled in through a flotilla of these lobster floats scattered just offshore from the Yankee Clipper Inn. Landing right at the inn was not something that I recommend. The ocean swell that seemed so gentle just offshore crushed the bow of my kayak onto the rough rocks and slammed me in the back of my legs as I struggled ashore. I suggest using a great sheltered public launch ramp at Pigeon Cove, just a couple of minutes' walk down the road, which is where I should have landed. This landing illustrated the challenges of paddling around Cape Ann. The power of the water may seem under control, but it is always just below the surface waiting to pounce on the unwary paddler.

Despite the difficult landing area in front of the Yankee Clipper Inn, this waterfront resort is a perfect spot to stay on a soft paddling escape to Cape Ann. Within easy walking distance of the heart of the village of Rockport, the Yankee Clipper is just far enough out of the village to feel secluded. Two buildings set in immaculate lawns perched on the edge of the ocean make up the Yankee Clipper Inn.

The two waterfront buildings date from different eras. The Main Inn is an imposing 1929 Art Deco masterpiece surrounded by manicured lawns and coastal gardens that flow down to the rocky shoreline. Breakfast is served here in the Veranda dining room from which almost every seat has a view of the ocean. You can plan your day's paddle based on how rough the water looks while you eat, and then relax with your coffee or tea. The Quarterdeck, set in the gardens and lawns, is a newer building that offers stunning vistas out over the oceans from most of its rooms. The staff are extremely helpful and friendly, making any time spent here very enjoyable.

There are several excellent paddling trips around Cape Ann. The best spot to start most of these trips is Rockport Harbor at the North Shore Kayak Outdoor Center. If you bring your own kayak, there are several public launch ramps around Cape Ann. A wheeled kayak cart would be a very handy item on a paddling trip

The tall stone tower of one of the twin lighthouses on Thacher Island has guided sailors since 1861.

here since none of the inns and B&Bs are directly on good launching points. It is possible to paddle from some of them but I don't recommend it. I will describe all paddling routes as if you are starting from the North Shore Outdoor Kayak Center, and you can adjust for that in your own plans if you do bring your own kayak.

As previously mentioned, Rockport Harbor is divided up into several separate areas like rooms, and each room has a different type of boat anchored in it. Furthest from the open water, reached by a narrow entrance and completely surrounded by huge cut-stone blocks, is the section of the harbor where the fishing boats moor. A bit further out, the harbor splits in two directions, one side of the channel for larger yachts and sailboats and the other side for small sailing dinghies; this is the area where the North Shore Kayak Outdoor Center launches and lands.

The most obvious plan for a day's paddle is to head for the three islands off Cape Ann. Straitsmouth Island, Thacher Island, and Milk Island lie in an arc following the coastline of Cape Ann south. First you will come to Straitsmouth Island, a little more than a mile (2 km) from Rockport. In the narrow channel between the island and the mainland, if the wind direction and the wave direction are right, there are generally some good compressed swells to surf on. If you don't like steep waves, you might prefer to round the island on the ocean side. The lighthouse is located on the northeastern tip of the island, and the surface of the water around the island is littered with dozens of multicolored lobster trap floats.

When you pass by Straitsmouth Island, the twin towers of Thacher Island will come into view. These two 123-foot (37.5 m) stone towers have been warning mariners of the dangers of coming too close to this island since 1861. They replace earlier 45-foot (14 m) twin towers that were built in 1771. Thacher Island is named for Anthony Thacher, a very unlucky settler whose ship was wrecked on this island in 1635. He lost his four children, twenty-one friends and relatives, and all of his possessions. Only he and his wife survived the wreck. The British government granted him the island, but he had no desire to live where he had lost so much, and he chose instead to live on the mainland in Marblehead.

Milk Island is a low rise of gravel and rock southwest of Thacher Island. It is not permissible to land on Milk Island, as it is a bird nesting sanctuary. Thousands and thousands of gulls, terns, and other seabirds circle this island all the time. There are so many that from a distance it looks hazy over parts of the island with thousands of gulls rising and falling on the air currents. The southeast corner of Milk Island projects a shallow shelf out into the rough waters of the Atlantic, creating very rough conditions even on calm days. On windy days this is not a good spot to be paddling!

Milk Island is shaped like a heart with the indent at the top of the heart facing northwest. This shallow bay offers a sheltered calm area to relax and catch your breath before the return paddle to Rockport. On your way back, check out the opposite side of the island that you passed on the way out. A possible side-trip on the way back into Rockport would be a paddle out to the Salvages, two mostly submerged ledges north of Straitsmouth Island. If you do paddle out to the Salvages, be wary of being dropped by a wave on the ledges, and keep a keen lookout for seals. Gray Harbor seals are often sighted out here but they are very shy.

Heading north out of Rockport Harbor you will paddle past several tiny protected harbors. These refuges with their huge cut-stone granite walls once sheltered fishing fleets but now they are filled with pleasure craft. Just north of Pigeon Cove the shoreline is dominated by huge bare expanses of granite running down into the sea. In a north breeze this is a very rough area to paddle. You will be sheltered from westerly winds until you reach Halibut Point State Park. A local fisherman hauling up his lobster traps off this point on a very calm day told me that Halibut Point really means "haul about point" but the mapmakers and creators of the park didn't understand the local dialect and thought the fishermen were calling the point "halibut point." I too could not really tell whether the fisherman was saying "haul about" or "halibut," but "haul about" makes far more sense, as this would be where the sailing vessels would change tack for the run down into Boston.

Halibut Point State Park is the site of a former quarry, and the shoreline here is a jumble of huge slabs on which the waves throw up spray even on a calm day and where the water fountains into the air in huge geysers on a windy day. It is not possible to land here safely, but there is a trail along the water's edge from Pigeon Cove to Halibut Point State Park. I would highly recommend this walk when you want to take a break from paddling. A round-trip hike from the Yankee Clipper Inn will take you a couple of hours. This trail is not on public land but there is an old right-of-way agreement with local landowners that allows walkers to pass along the water's edge. Please respect the local residents' privacy and stay on the trail.

Once around Halibut Point, you will see small Folly Cove open up before you. It is possible to land at the steep cobblestone beach at the end of the cove, where you will see a small parking spot and a bench for a snack break. As you continue down the shore of Cape Ann, you will pass three more small harbors, all with huge breakwaters around them, before you come to the lighthouse that marks the entrance to the Annisquam River. This newly restored lighthouse anchored to a slice of granite on the point has guided boats into the channel to the river for 200 years. It also gives a good warning to kayakers.

Past the Annisquam light, motorboats, sailboats, and all manner of personal watercraft are moving up and down the river. I would suggest that the lighthouse is a good place to turn around and head back to Rockport. If you have taken your time exploring or have paddled into any of the small harbors along the way, you will have had a full day of paddling by the time you return to Rockport anyway.

Although it is possible to continue on up the Annisquam River, through the canal linking the river to Gloucester Harbor, and then from Gloucester Harbor to continue back up the coast to Rockport, I do not recommend this trip. This circumnavigation of Cape Ann is a long paddle in widely varying conditions and should only be attempted by the very experienced paddler.

There are several problem areas on the paddle between the mouth of the Annisquam River and the eastern shore of Cape Ann. The first is the traffic on the river itself. During the summer, this is a very busy waterway and it is really not much fun to paddle in a kayak. The second area of concern is the current in Blynman Canal, which leads from the Annisquam River out into Gloucester Harbor. This current is at its slowest at slack tide, but on either side of slack tide it can give quite a bumpy ride. If you happened to time your paddle wrong and were facing an opposing current, I'm not sure that you would be able to make any headway against the tide. If you reach the narrowest part of the canal — the section under the bridge leading out into Gloucester Harbor — when the tidal current is flushing out into the harbor, you will need fairly well developed whitewater skills to ride the waves out into the harbor.

The third problem area on this route is Gloucester Harbor itself. The large commercial fishing fleet, growing numbers of tour boats and whale-watching boats, and the seemingly endless parade of private pleasure boats turn this harbor into a dangerous place to paddle. In my mind, this is the most difficult and dangerous paddling of any place mentioned in this book solely because of the boat traffic. If you do decide to do this paddle, the last challenge to overcome after the boat traffic, currents, and even more boat traffic, is facing the power of the open North Atlantic at the end of a strenuous day. The stretch of coast from the Dog Bar Breakwater, which shelters Gloucester Harbor all the way up to Rockport, is very rugged with very few places to land or even find shelter to relax in a bit of calm water.

You could shorten the paddle by staying at the Samarkand B&B at the southern end of Good Harbor Beach. With its shared bathrooms and simple, clean accommodations, this B&B is more like a family cottage or home than an inn. It has a friendly atmosphere and easy water access. From here it is a short half-day paddle back to Rockport.

Cape Ann is bursting with activities other than kayaking. If you still crave something active, the mountain biking here is challenging, and the trails lead through some beautiful countryside. The roads are great for road cycling, and this is perhaps the best way to explore the towns of Rockport and Gloucester from your inn. The Rockport galleries are very attractive, and Gloucester's long maritime history can be explored in its museums. If you want to try paddling in another area close to Cape Ann, Essex River Adventures offers guided sea kayak tours on the Essex River and surrounding areas.

INN INFO

Yankee Clipper Inn ★ ★ ★
P.O. Box 2399
Granite Street
Rockport, MA 01966
1-800-545-3699
978-546-9730
Fax: 978-546-9730
www.yankeeclipperinn.com

Samarkand Inn ★ ★
1 Harbor Road
Gloucester, MA 01930
978-283-3757
www.cape-ann.com/samarkand

FOR FURTHER INFORMATION
www.cape-ann.com

MAPS AND CHARTS
NOAA # 13279 at 1:20,000

RENTAL/OUTFITTERS

North Shore Kayak Outdoor Center
9 Tuna Wharf
Rockport, MA 01966
978-546-5050
www.northshorekayak.com

Essex River Basin Adventures
66R Main St.
Essex, MA
768-ERBA
1-800-KAYAK-04

TRAVEL INFO
Cape Ann can be reached by train or car. The staff at the Yankee Clipper Inn will meet you at the train station if you give them advance warning.

Martha's Vineyard: A Victorian Island Escape

All islands have a certain mystique, but Martha's Vineyard has a personality all its own as a favorite resort destination for people wanting to escape to the seashore. The Steamship Authority operates regular ferry service to both Vineyard Haven and Oak Bluffs. Both destinations should be part of any paddling trip on the island. Before you go to Martha's Vineyard, decide if you want to take your car over. It is not necessary, but it does make getting to the put-in points much easier. If you decide not to take your car — I don't, myself — a kayak cart will be a great aid in getting your craft to and from the water.

If you take the ferry across Vineyard Sound to Vineyard Haven, you could put in at the launching spot conveniently located right beside the ferry dock in Vineyard Haven. You could then paddle to Oak Bluffs. But do this paddle only if the wind is westerly. An east wind on this coast will generate large unfriendly waves and make an otherwise enjoyable paddle a dangerous chore.

The weather here can change very quickly. I had decided to paddle over from Woods Hole to Martha's Vineyard because the weather looked good. The tide was running in my favor, and I did not want to wait for the next ferry and have to carry my fully loaded kayak to the ferry and then from the ferry to a launch point or to the inn on the island side. Paddling out of Woods Hole was fine, except for the heavy boat traffic and the difficulty of launching close to the ferry docks. Once I rounded the point and headed for the distant shore of Martha's Vineyard, I was heading into quartering seas of 4 to 5 feet (1.5–2 m) from the west cutting across 4-foot (1.5 m) ocean swells of from the east. Not a pleasant combination for a 4-mile (6.5 km) paddle, but I foolishly persevered. After all, it was sunny and there was no real wind to speak of.

That changed about a mile (2 km) offshore. The sky became dark quite quickly, and a strong west wind blew in. This wind whipped up the waves from the west and created a very confused sea as well as adding to my drift parallel to the shore of Martha's Vineyard. What had seemed a bit more than an hour's paddle was rapidly become a lot of hard work. Stroke, brace, stroke, brace, paddle stroke brace,

brace — these words defined my world for the next two hours as I fought increasing wind and seas across Vineyard Sound. Finally, I rounded the West Chop and had a break from the wind and the worst of the wind-driven waves. As I struggled past the breakwater into the harbor at Vineyard Haven, I had a true sense of why this place should be called a haven. I paddled up to the beach beside the ferry dock just as a ferry was pulling in — the third to arrive since I had left Woods Hole. I would have been far wiser to have waited for the ferry and spent my time exploring the coast of Martha's Vineyard by kayak.

In Vineyard Haven there are several B&Bs, most of which are on Main Street a block uphill from the beach. But because of the distance between these places and the water, and because the harbor is so busy, I only spend a short amount of time in Vineyard Haven when I'm on Martha's Vineyard. There is a kayak rental shop in Vineyard Haven, and if you did not bring your own kayak over this is an excellent place to base yourself for exploring the eastern coast of the island.

Perhaps the best B&B in Vineyard Haven is Martha's Place, a delightfully restored mansion on the hill overlooking the harbor, just steps from all the shops and restaurants in Vineyard Haven. There are several other B&Bs alongside Martha's Place, all of which offer excellent accommodations in a variety of styles and price ranges.

Paddling near Vineyard Haven includes trips into Lagoon Pond, a deep saltwater pond reaching into the interior of the island from Vineyard Haven Harbor. Although there is very little public land on the shores of the pond, it is possible to access the pond from the harbor under a bridge just inside the eastern breakwater, and from a public launch site just off Beach Road. The kayak rental shop Wind's Up! is located along this stretch of road dividing Lagoon Pond from Vineyard Haven Harbor.

Paddling around the harbor itself is a journey through yachting history. There is every type of sailing craft here, mostly old wooden classics but some newer boats as well as large schooners. While I was here I found the friends from New Zealand that I had last seen in Mystic Seaport, on their 57-foot yawl, *Sina*, moored just inside the breakwater. They were five years into their trip around the world and figured they had a couple of years to go yet before they returned to New Zealand. The scale of their trip put my short weekend on Martha's Vineyard into perspective.

Just south of Vineyard Haven, around the point called East Chop, on the eastern shore of Martha's Vineyard, is the very protected harbor of Oak Bluffs surrounded by a Victorian gingerbread fantasy. The town of Oak Bluffs had its origin in the camp meetings of the Methodist revival in the nineteenth century. In the late 1800s a flurry of construction resulted in cottages and homes that fairly drip gingerbread. The meandering streets and paths — many closed to motor traffic —

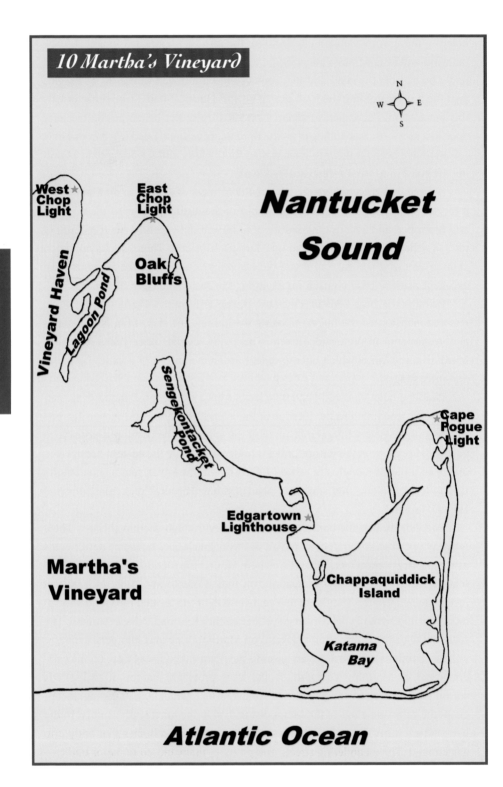

10 *Martha's Vineyard*

N
W E
S

West Chop Light

East Chop Light

Oak Bluffs

Nantucket Sound

Vineyard Haven

Lagoon Pond

Sengekontacket Pond

Cape Pogue Light

Edgartown Lighthouse

Martha's Vineyard

Chappaquiddick Island

Katama Bay

Atlantic Ocean

MASSACHUSETTS

connect to circular commons surrounded by quaint Victorian cottages adorned with every manner of filagree and trim imaginable painted in a wide variety of colors. These circular commons mimic the circles of tents in the original Methodist revival meetings. It is truly a charming village with the candy-colored gingerbread homes looking like something out of a fairy tale.

Unless you take your car on the ferry or have a kayak cart to wheel your kayak around, the easiest way to arrive in Oak Bluffs is by kayak from Vineyard Haven. But the ferry wharf at Oak Bluffs is outside the harbor and has no easy landing sites close to the wharf. So your landing spot in Oak Bluffs will depend on where you decide to stay.

Right on the harbor is the Wesley Hotel. This grand old lady of island hotels dominates the harbor, but is not as easy to access from kayak as it is from a larger boat. The sea wall of the harbor prevents a kayaker from landing directly in front of the hotel, but there is a small dock for yacht tenders in the southeast corner of the harbor. You can land your kayak there and then carry it across the street to the Wesley Hotel. Ask the hotel staff where you can store your boat while off the water.

The lobby of the Wesley still has a gracious Victorian presence, but the renovations to the rooms have removed their historical character. The accommodations are quite adequate, however, ideally located for walking through the village, and close to all the restaurants. This is also one of the few places we've been to that offer smoking rooms.

Other accommodations for paddlers planning to kayak out of Oak Bluffs are three B&Bs side by side along Seaview Avenue, just across the road from the ocean and beach. The Oak House B&B, the Beach House B&B, and the Capricorn House on the Beach all offer unique Victorian accommodation and sumptuous breakfasts. During the months of July and August you must land south of the last breakwater on this beach to be legal, but for the rest of the year you can land and launch directly in front of the B&Bs. These B&Bs are just south of the ferry wharf, a block or so south of the large public park, where frequent concerts are held in the summer months.

There are many excellent spots to paddle on Martha's Vineyard, but I will concentrate on the area between Vineyard Haven and Chappaquiddick Island. This area offers the most sheltered paddling on the island and has plenty to offer any weekend paddler. The south shore of Martha's Vineyard, on the other hand, is completely exposed to the wide-open Atlantic Ocean and has some very hazardous dumping surf.

If you get an early enough start, a paddle out to the tip of Cape Pogue and around the large lagoon encircled by the Cape makes a great full-day trip. It is about 20 miles (32 km) round-trip, so be sure to give yourself lots of time and pack a lunch for a picnic out on the sands of Cape Pogue. Or, if you don't want to take a picnic, you could stop in Edgartown for lunch. Bring a cable lock to secure your kayak while you are eating in Edgartown. Theft is not a real problem, but if your kayak cannot be moved, then no inquisitive child can act on the temptation to try paddling away in your craft.

Head south from Oak Bluffs along the sweeping curve of the shoreline. The beach by Oak Bluffs, the one you will launch from if you are staying in the one of the B&Bs, is protected on the southern end by a rock breakwater stretching out into the water. At high tide these rocks are mostly covered, and a kayak can slip over the deeper rocks and coast along the shore. I saw several wood ducks, loons, cormorants, and bufflehead ducks in this short stretch of coastline between the end of the Oak Bluffs Beach and the entrance to Sengekontacket Pond.

If you are a birder or a wildlife buff, this shoreline and Sengekontacket Pond will probably occupy you for the entire day. You will find the north entrance into Sengekontacket Pond under a small bridge that supports the road from Oak Bluffs to Edgartown along the coast. On the Nantucket Sound side of the road is State Beach, a long crescent of sand crammed with sunbathers from July to Labor Day and largely deserted the rest of the year. On the inland side of the road is Senge-kontacket Pond. For over 2 miles (3 km) this pond parallels the ocean, separated from it only by the strip of sand on which the road runs.

As you enter the pond, you will either have to fight the tidal current or be pushed into the pond. The banks close to the entrance channels are generally lined with fishermen, so watch that you don't get tangled in their fishing lines. Much of the shoreline of Sengekontacket Pond is marsh and provides nesting habitat for many different types of waterfowl. Early spring and fall are the best times to paddle here for birdwatching.

The only concerns with paddling in the pond are personal watercraft, which zip around like annoying mosquitos on the weekends, and the tidal currents under the bridges leading from the open water into Sengekontacket Pond. These currents can throw up standing waves and are quite fun to paddle down but are a lot of work to paddle up. If you are paddling across the current, remember to lean downstream in the same direction as the current. This will stop the tendency of your kayak to be turned over by the pressure of the current against the bottom.

Leaving Sengekontacket Pond through the opening under the southern bridge, you will find yourself near the end of the publicly owned State beach. As you continue south you will pass a number of small changing houses along the shore. These are private and are owned by the homes set back from the water. Do not go above the low water line here if you do have to land, as Massachusetts is one of only two states where private property remains private to the low water line. The

The houses in Oak Bluffs drip with gingerbread.

beach slowly peters out and homes move closer to the waterfront as you proceed further along the shore.

There is a very shallow bay just before you turn around the point into Edgartown. The long, hooked sand spit forming the eastern edge of the bay is a great stopping spot if you need to get out and stretch your legs. Try not to disturb the grass and other plants in the sand just at the back of the beach. This is a sensitive ecological zone and can be easily damaged by thoughtless walkers. Keep an eye out for piping plovers along this stretch. I do not know if they nest here but I have seen them scurrying along the shoreline in this area. This beach runs almost due south and ends in the tiny spit of land on which the Edgartown lighthouse stands.

Edgartown Harbor is the narrow part of a passage leading from Nantucket Sound into Katama Bay. If the weather is a bit windy or if you have already explored Cape Pogue, Katama Bay is worth the long paddle. There are several narrow inlets off the bay and the south end of the bay is separated from the Atlantic by a very narrow strip of sand. This sand strip is the back side of Katama Beach, and it is possible to land and walk over to see the surf pounding in on the exposed shore. If you decide to go swimming or paddling in this surf be wary of the undertows here. They can be quite strong.

Cape Pogue is a long strip of sand wrapped around Chappaquiddick Island protecting the island from the Atlantic Ocean and Nantucket Sound. The Cape Pogue Lighthouse is located at the extreme northern tip of the barrier sand dunes. Most of this area, from the narrow entrance to Cape Pogue Bay to Dyke Bridge — which connects the barrier beaches to Chappaquiddick Island — is encompassed by the Cape Pogue Wildlife Refuge. Most visitors know this area for the long stretches of barrier beaches, but kayakers with a naturalist bent will appreciate the salt marsh, fresh and brackish ponds, and red cedar uplands that provide homes for nesting terns and shorebirds, upland game birds and songbirds, small mammals, and white-tailed deer. If you are lucky you may see osprey, which use this area as a nesting and feeding area in the summer months.

From Edgartown, paddle east along the northern shore of Chappaquiddick Island toward the narrow entrance to Cape Pogue Bay. This entrance is called the Cape Pogue Gut and can have strong tidal currents running through it. Use caution when entering and exiting the bay. The water inside the bay is very rich in shellfish. It provides almost half of the Massachusetts scallop harvest. At the northeast corner of Cape Pogue Bay is the entrance into Shear Pen Pond, and at the southeast end of the bay is the long narrow channel leading down between the barrier dune beach and Chappaquiddick Island to Poucha Pond. It is possible to get landlocked while paddling down to Poucha Pond if you do not time the tides right.

Nantucket Sound has only a 2-foot (.6 m) tidal range or so, but that is plenty to paddle a kayak in. If you want to get out and stretch your legs, the hike up to the lighthouse is well worth the walk. Look for a suitable landing spot on the northern barrier dunes. In nesting times some areas are closed to people to allow shore birds to nest in peace, so make sure that you are landing in a legal spot. These closed areas change from year to year as the birds move their nests, so it is up to you to make sure that you are not doing any damage when you land. Pull your kayaks well above high tide or, if you can't do that, tie them off to something solid. It would be a long, long walk back to the inn from here. There is one place to stay right out here on the tip of Cape Pogue. The Jib is a home that you can rent at certain times of the year.

The Cape Pogue lighthouse is Martha's Vineyards most remote lighthouse. The only way to get here is by boat or special off-road sand vehicles. Permits for the off-road vehicles are very expensive so it is possible to have the area to yourself sometimes. Set back 300 feet from the ocean, the lighthouse was built in 1922, the last in a long succession of lighthouses washed away by the hungry sea. This building was moved to its present location in 1985 when the waves started to threaten it. Believe it or not, it was moved in one piece by a helicopter, lifted up and gently lowered by a big hand from the sky.

The Wesley Hotel rises above the harbor in Oak Bluffs.

The return trip to Oak Bluffs can be a long paddle, so make sure you leave yourself plenty of time to get home. There is plenty enough paddling on Martha's Vineyard to satisfy any paddler for several days, but the areas I have singled out here are not-to-be-missed destinations.

If you want a change from paddling around the island, think about cycling on the island. Martha's Vineyard is very bicycle-friendly and has wonderful bike and inline skating paths crisscrossing the island. Bikes are available for rent in almost every town and at most places that rent kayaks. The hiking and walking on the island is quite varied, from forested bluffs to beaches — and, of course, the beach is always there to relax on. For those of you interested in antiques, Martha's Vineyard seems to have antique stores located around every corner. Finally, just walking around Oak Bluffs and taking in the richly embellished Victorian gingerbread architecture is a great way to spend an afternoon.

INN INFO

The Wesley Hotel ★ ★ ★
70 Lake Avenue, P.O. Box 2370
Oak Bluffs, Martha's Vineyard
MA 02557
508-693-6611
Fax: 508-693-5389
www.wesleyhotel.vineyard.net

The Capricorn House on the Beach ★ ★ ★ ★
79 Seaview Avenue, P.O. Box 855
Oak Bluffs, Martha's Vineyard
MA 02557
Phone and fax: 508-693-2848
www.capricornhouse.com

The Beach House Bed and Breakfast on the Ocean ★ ★ ★ ★
P.O. Box 417
Oak Bluffs, Martha's Vineyard
MA 02557
508-693-3955
www.beachhousemv.com

The Oak House ★ ★ ★ ★
Seaview Avenue, P.O. Box 299
Oak Bluffs, Martha's Vineyard
MA 02557
1-800-245-5979
508-693-4187
Fax: 508-696-7385
E-mail: inns@vineyard.net
www.vineyard.net/inns

The Jib Cape Pogue
http://people.ne.mediaone.net/bcosler/index.html

MAPS & CHARTS

Waterproof Charts, # 10
or NOAA chart # 13233

RENTALS

East Coast Outfitters kayak rentals & tours 508-693-8993
Kasoon Kayak Company 508-627-2553
Martha's Vineyard Kayak Company 508-627-0151
Wind's Up! windsurfing instruction and rentals 508-693-4252

TRAVEL INFO

Easiest access is by ferry as a foot passenger. If you want to take your car, be sure to make a reservation. The ferry can be completely full on long weekends. It is also possible to take a bus to the island. The island has a small airport.

ISLAND ACCESS

www.islandferry.com
Steamship transport:
508-477-8600 or 508-693-9130
Bonanza Bus Lines:
1-800-556-3815
Martha's Vineyard Airport:
508-693-7022

MASSACHUSETTS

VERMONT

Tranquility on Lake Champlain

Often called the Sixth Great Lake, or New England's "West Coast," Lake Champlain is a large and diverse body of water that offers a wide variety of sea kayaking possibilities. There is something here for all paddlers, from first-timers to long-time experts. The same section of lake can be dead calm one day and a washing machine of big rollers and churning waves the next day. No matter what the weather, though, Lake Champlain always seems to infuse some tranquility into those who paddle here. The shoreline changes from pastoral to rugged in the space of a mile (2 km) and then back to pastoral. From almost anywhere on the lake, you can see the mountains in Vermont or the silhouettes of the Adirondacks in New York. Lake Champlain is bordered by Vermont, New York, and Quebec, and its waters flow north into the Richelieu River in Quebec.

Several million years ago, Lake Champlain was a long shallow extension of the Atlantic Ocean and contained coral reefs and ancient species of fish and whales. In fact, the oldest known fossils of coral reefs in the world, around 500 million years old, have been found in the limestone and shale coast of Lake Champlain. The fossilized "Charlotte Whale," for example, a whale related to the present-day Beluga, was discovered in 1849 under 10 feet (3 m) of thick clay. Some of the freshwater fish found in the lake today have direct ancestral ties to ocean-dwelling species. After the last ice age, the land rose again as the glaciers withdrew, and the channel flowing north out of the lake was formed.

Lake Champlain has dozens of great paddling destinations, but I am going to focus on paddling trips off North Hero Island. North Hero and South Hero Islands divide the northern section of the lake into two parts, that run north and south. (Grand Isle is the larger northern half of South Hero Island.) Lying offshore from these islands are a few other islands, some private and some public. There are four islands to the east of North Hero, one of which — Knight Island — is a state park. To the west lies the large island of Isle La Motte, and jutting southward between these two is the Alburg Peninsula. North Hero Island is almost cut in half parallel to the tip of the Alburg Peninsula. All of these islands and the channels between them make for excellent sea kayaking.

The Hero Islands acquired their name from a land grant made by the newly independent Republic of Vermont to Ethan Allen and his brother Ira. Ethan Allen was a revolutionary war hero and leader of Vermont's Green Mountain Boys. He wrote to Vermont from England, where he was a war prisoner, asking that these islands be granted to himself and the Green Mountain Boys, and that they be named the Heroes in honor of his brother and himself. He seems to have had a pretty good opinion of himself! The petition for the land was granted in 1779, and many of the Green Mountain Boys settled on the islands after the American Revolutionary War.

Isle La Motte is named for Captain Sieur de La Motte, the commander of the French Carignan regiment, which built Fort Ste. Anne, the first white settlement in Vermont, in 1666. The Abenaki Natives had a village of around 500 inhabitants on the south end of South Hero when it was first observed by white explorers. Now, North and South Hero are sleepy islands with rolling pastures and some great waterfront accommodations. The best of these for a soft paddling trip is Shore Acres Inn and Restaurant. Shore Acres is a twenty-three-room inn located on

The Green Mountains are visible across Lake Champlain from the grounds of Shore Acres.

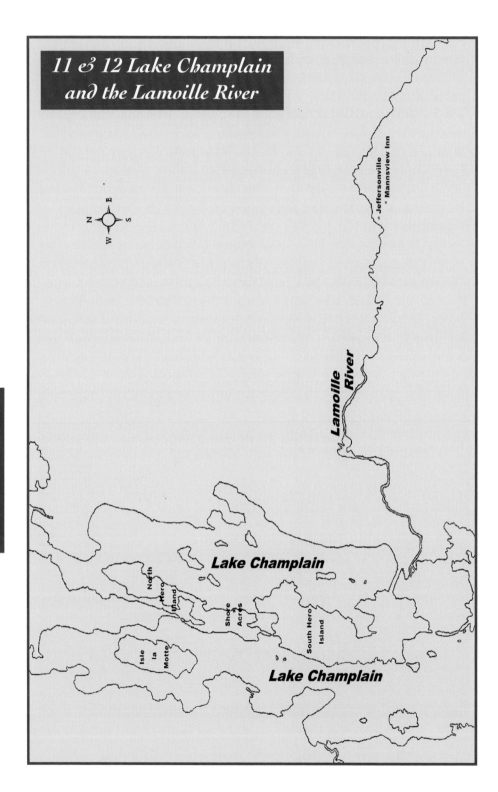

11 & 12 Lake Champlain
and the Lamoille River

Jeffersonville
Mannsview Inn

Lamoille River

Lake Champlain

North Hero Island

Shore Acres

South Hero Island

Isle la Motte

Lake Champlain

50 acres (20 hectares) of land with half a mile (1 km) of private shoreline. All the rooms except four are waterfront rooms that look east over the Inland Sea toward the Green Mountains of Vermont. It is located just a few miles south of the village of North Hero, where the local general store, Hero's Welcome, rents kayaks.

You can launch from Shore Acres either straight off the east shore or a little further north, where there is a small cove with a pebble beach. The best spot off the east shore is near the base of a large tree with its roots running into the water. Landing options change as the water level fluctuates over the course of a season. The best spot to leave your boat close to the water is off the little pebble beach north of the Shore Acres buildings.

The waters surrounding the Hero Islands offer several types of paddling. Directly offshore from Shore Acres is the big water of the Inland Sea. The Inland Sea encompasses some of the most diverse paddling on the lake. Not only are there extensive protected bays like the contained water found in the Gut, but there are many islands and marshes to explore, as well as stretches of open water. The water on the west side of the Heroes is known as the Broad Lake. This long, deep section of the lake extends from Canada south to the narrows by Split Rock Mountain. The area of the Broad Lake described here is somewhat sheltered by Cumberland Head, which juts out from the New York shoreline about halfway down the length of South Hero Island. This is still a challenging piece of water to paddle due to the shoreline cliffs that reflect waves and do not allow for safe landing.

One other possible water hazard is "Champ," Lake Champlain's version of the Loch Ness Monster. The existence of Champ is still unproven, but every year there are dozens of sightings of an unknown sea creature in the waters of Lake Champlain. Since the time of the Abenaki and the Iroquois in the Champlain Lowlands, there have been legends of the Great Horned Serpent. Their depictions resemble the descriptions given by modern-day witnesses. All have described a creature measuring 15 to 30 feet long (5–10 m) with a long, serpentine neck and one to five humps on its back. Keep an eye out, but if you do see Champ be aware that he/she is protected by law in New York and Vermont. Both states have passed resolutions protecting the mysterious monster. The only place where Champ can still be hunted down is in the area of the lake that lies in Quebec. The Canadian government has yet to enact any legal protection.

Although the paddling options here are almost endless, I especially recommend two daytrips. The first is a simple circumnavigation of the north half of North Hero Island. North Hero is almost cut in half by a narrow isthmus at Carry Bay. I imagine it got its name from the easy portage from one side of the island to the other — the portage is just the width of the road. At very low water levels, it might even be possible to work your way through the culvert under the road.

From Shore Acres, paddle north along the shore of North Hero Island. About a mile and a half (3 km) north you will come to the bay that forms North Hero Harbor. In the harbor there are usually moored boats, ranging from fishing boats to sleek sailboats. The entire village of North Hero is spread out along the shore with the road running through it. Once you paddle out of the harbor and head north again, you will have another half mile (1 km) or so to where you can lift over into Carry Bay. The guardrails on the road can make it a bit difficult if you are alone but they should present no obstacle for two people.

Once into Carry Bay, follow the north shore as it curves around to a point. Between the point and the mainland is the Alburg Passage. This fairly narrow channel leads north between the Alburg Peninsula and the west shore of North Hero Island. At its narrowest point, a bridge crosses it, carrying Route 2 south onto the island. On the mainland side of the bridge is the village of South Alburg. This is your last chance to stop until you get back to North Hero, so if you are hungry and short on snacks and didn't stop at the Hero's Welcome General Store in North Hero, this is the place to stock up.

Boat traffic can be quite busy through here in the summer time. The narrow channel is the most sheltered way to the northern corner of the lake, so many fishermen in small boats use it. Once past the bridge, the passage opens up and after a half a mile or so (1 km) the shore of North Hero starts curving away to the east. Follow this shore until it ends in a point. Hog Island is just over a half a mile (1 km) to the north. North of that is Missisquoi Bay, which is shallow and largely a protected nature sanctuary.

Whether you decide to paddle up into Missisquoi Bay will be determined by the weather, the time of day, and how much energy you have. This is the halfway point if you are heading back to Shore Acres. If you paddle into the bay you will double the distance you need to paddle. It is about 5 miles (8 km) south along the east shore of North Hero Island back to the inn. The north half of North Hero Island is much wilder than further south. There are few roads, and much of the shoreline seems deserted. There are some private campgrounds and cottages but very little commercial development. It is a pastoral landscape that you paddle by on your return to the inn.

For a second daytrip from Shore Acres, consider paddling around the south half of North Hero Island. In order to make the paddle the same length as the previous route and to avoid paddling over the same ground twice, I would recommend paddling out and around Knight Island on your way up to the lift-over spot into Carry Bay. Knight Island is a state park and has hiking trails and campsites on its shores. Just paddling out to it and hiking its trails would be a great way to spend a day.

Hero's Welcome is the heart of the village of North Hero. It carries everything from food to nautical charts.

The east shore of Knight Island is very overgrown, with few campsites and pullouts to stop at. Looking east, you'll see the Green Mountains rise up in layers of green, blue, and gray. The crossing to Knight Island is the most exposed water mentioned in this section on Lake Champlain. Waves can build quite rapidly here as water and wind get funneled through the Gut. Be aware of the wind and weather conditions when paddling out to Knight Island. From the north end of Knight Island it is just over a half a mile (1 km) in a straight line to the lift-over into Carry Bay.

Once in Carry Bay, head for the long white line on the far side of the bay. As you paddle closer to this line, you will recognize it as a railway embankment of the old Rutland Railway, made out of huge slabs of white marble. There is a break in the embankment almost due west of the lift-over spot into Carry Bay. In order to paddle all the way around Hero you must get on the west side of this embankment. The large deep bay opening up to the south on the east side of the embankment ends in a swamp about a half a mile (1 km) south.

When you get to the western side of the embankment, follow it south until the old railway line turns inland. At this point, the shoreline consists of limestone cliffs rising in uniform layers out of the cold water. There is nowhere to land in case of an emergency, and in windy weather the waves reflected off the cliff face make for some very challenging paddling. Normally, however, it is possible to glide along just a few feet offshore, with the cliffs and cedars clinging to them rising overhead. There are cottages here, but most of them are not visible because they are on top of the cliff. The only real signs of human habitation are the various types of docks, stairs, and ladders by which the cottagers access the water. In spring and early summer, many of these ladders and stairs are still twisted and bent from the power of the winter season's ice. This stretch of shoreline is a great spot to watch for cliff swallows and other cliff-nesting birds.

As you turn east around the final cliff face on North Hero Island, another long white marble block embankment bars your way into the Gut. It is almost half a mile (1 km) from the last cliff to the opening in the old railway embankment and the calm waters of the Gut. In the Gut there are usually dozens of small boats bobbing in the water with silent fishermen hunkered over their poles. On rare occasions there will be a lot of boat traffic here but it is generally not a problem. Looking east across the Gut, you will see a bridge. The route back to Shore Acres lies under this bridge. Just to the west of the bridge is a small park where you can stop and stretch if you need a break. Once under the bridge, turn north and follow the shoreline back to Shore Acres. If he sees you, Cooper the dog will probably welcome you back to the inn.

Off-the-water activities can be divided into those available at Shore Acres and those available locally. Shore Acres offers tennis, swimming, and a practice nine-hole golf course — and lots of very comfortable Adirondack chairs scattered around the grounds, which are perfect for curling up with a good book. There are also several area attractions off the property. You could rent a bike for the day in North Hero and explore the islands, drive across to the mainland and visit Ben and Jerry's ice cream plant, or you could wander through the streets of nearby Burlington. Perhaps the most unique event available on weekends in the summer is a chance to see the famous "dancing" Royal Lipizzan stallions, just south of Shore Acres on North Hero.

INN INFO

**Shore Acres Inn and
Restaurant** ★ ★ ★ ★
237 Shore Acres Drive
North Hero Island
VT 05474
802-372-8722
www.shoreacres.com
info@shoreacres.com

North Hero House ★ ★ ★ ★
P.O. Box 207
North Hero, VT 05474
802-372-4732
1-888-525-3644
Fax: 802-372-3218
www.northherohouse.com
nhhlake@aol.com

RENTALS

Hero's Welcome General Store
1-800-372-HERO
Fax: 802-372-3205
www.heroswelcome.com
Camphero@AOL.com

MAPS

NOAA Waterproof Chart, # 12
(2-sided chart of northern Lake
Champlain — Burlington to
Richelieu River)
Call 1-800-423-9026 or
www.waterproofcharts.com
Also available at Hero's Welcome
General Store.

TRAVEL INFO

Float plane access is possible
but this is really a drive-to
destination.

TRANQUILITY ON LAKE CHAMPLAIN

The Lamoille River: River Running and Antiques

It would be hard to design a more ideal soft paddling destination than the Mannsview Inn near the Smugglers Notch ski area. This white clapboard B&B just outside of Jeffersonville, Vermont, looks out over the Green Mountains but is not on the shores of any water. Why then, is this a perfect soft paddling destination? The answer can be found in the yard between the house and the large barn. The barn is now a huge antique center, but parked in the yard are trailers filled with canoes and kayaks. This is not just a comfortable B&B, this is the home of Smugglers Notch Canoe Touring. Kelly and Bette Mann operate the Mannsview Inn, Smugglers Notch Canoe Touring and the antique center. They offer packages that include your accommodations, canoe rental, and shuttle service. All you have to do is show up ready to paddle and they will take care of the rest. After a day's paddle on the river you might like to relax in the outdoor spa. Don't do this before going out for dinner, however, as it is very difficult to get motivated to go in search of a meal after a soak in the hot tub.

Paddling here by canoe or kayak is focused on the Lamoille River, which was named in the 1600s by the French explorer Samuel de Champlain, founder of Montreal and visitor to many of the other destinations in this book. The name has two possible origins. In the most popular version, Champlain wanted to name the river "la Moitte," because of the many gulls following the course of the river inland, but his cartographer forgot to cross the Ts on La Moitte. One problem with this version is that Champlain made most of his own maps and would likely have noticed the mistake. A more academic possibility involves the change of word usage and meaning in French. *La moelle* means "the marrow" in French, as in bone marrow. In the sixteenth and seventeenth centuries, the word *la moelle* also meant the center or middle, just as bone marrow is in the middle of the bone. The Lamoille River is the middle river of the three largest rivers that drain into Lake Champlain from the east. Samuel de Champlain could have named this middle river the La Moelle, which ultimately shifted to today's Lamoille. Whatever the story, a paddle on the Lamoille River valley will truly sink into the marrow of your soul.

Your paddling day starts off with a large breakfast served up by the Manns in their sunny kitchen area. After breakfast, drive your car to the take-out point on the river and the staff at Mannsview Inn will pick you up and drive you in their van with a canoe on top to your selected put-in spot. If you are planning to take the whole day to paddle, you might want to stop in Jeffersonville to pick up some food for a picnic. Bring plenty of water, as it can be very hot on the river and there is nowhere to get good water. Once you reach your put-in point and unload the canoe, it is simply a matter of paddling downstream to where you left your car. Stepping off the bank and into the canoe, you move into a different realm, where the most common animals seen are Vermont's legendary cows.

There are several lengths of trips possible, and you will be able to paddle different sections of the river on different days. As the level of skill needed for most trips is minimal, this is an excellent trip for first-time paddlers. The only time paddling may get more difficult is during the spring runoff when the melting snow raises the level of the river. This is more of a hazard when combined with the increased risk of hypothermia in extremely cold spring water. But from June through till the end of the paddling season in October the Lamoille River offers easy carefree paddling.

You pass through landscapes that change from forests of pine and maples to pastures, and there is very little development along the river to disturb the pastoral scenery. At every opening in the trees, the Green Mountains rise in blue and green layers framing the sky above you. The fall is a particularly magical time to paddle here. The hills and mountainsides flame scarlet and gold, mottled with the dark green of pines. Alongside the water, smaller maples seem to glow with an inner light in oranges and reds. Fall is a truly magical time to be here.

As the river loops through gravel bars, it occasionally builds up enough speed to get some adrenaline flowing, and then it settles down again to a slow meandering flow. There are a couple of falls and rapids to be wary of if you miss your take-out point. Smugglers Notch Canoe Touring has set out three distinct trips, which range from one to four hours of actual paddling time. There are other options and combinations available as well. Both Kelly and Bette know the area very well and have paddled all of the destinations they will send you to. When linking up various sections of the river, you may have to portage around some rapids. There are at least two large rapids/falls in the length of the river that Smugglers Notch Canoe Touring trips cover, but these lie between their regular trip routes. Both Cady's Falls and Dogshead Falls are delightful spots to picnic at but not to paddle over. Only if you miss your take-out point will you have to worry about these obstacles.

If you want to swim on your trip, the further upstream you are, the cleaner the water will be. For most of the river the water is quite clean, but there are a

Dogshed Falls is a wonderful spot to break for lunch. Make sure you don't paddle over it!

few areas close to farmers' fields and near dairy farms where the water quality could be a bit suspect. The only other hazard of paddling here is encountered on the shore, not in the canoe. Poison ivy is quite common in this area and I have seen it several times on the riverbanks as well as near one waterfall. Make sure you know how to identify this plant and keep well clear of it when you do see it. The other plants and wildlife you may see are not dangerous at all, so they can be fully enjoyed.

While paddling a stretch of this river I saw a dozen cedar waxwings flitting among the cedar trees beside the shore. Just before that a kingfisher had flown downstream ahead of us and a great blue heron had squawked angrily as he flew upstream with his slow, cumbersome wingbeats. The air was very quiet, white fluffy clouds floated overhead, and the mountains were a deep blue in the distance. The only sound I could hear was the chuckling of water along the sides of the canoe, the splash of my paddle, and the distant drone of a tractor. The poplar leaves fluttered showing the silvery bottom side of their leaves, and I leaned back and just let the canoe drift. What a perfect way to spend a day. I was gently jolted back to reality when the canoe grated on a gravel shoal and I had to get out to free it up.

All too soon the covered bridge that is just half a mile (1 km) from the take-out near Jeffersonville appeared around a bend in the river and this day's paddling was over. Pull your boat up on the beach and turn it over. The folks at Smugglers Notch Canoe tours will come and pick it up later. This is truly a paddling trip with no worries. Driving back to the inn you can stop for dinner in Jeffersonville or get back to the inn, freshen up, and head out to one of the forty restaurants that dot the area.

Lamoille County and the Green Mountains are alive with off-the-water activities. The hiking options can be either strenuous or relaxing, but either way the views are wonderful, with mountains layering back into the distance and quaint little towns nestled into the fold of a hill below you. At the top of the road running by the front of the Mannsview Inn is Smugglers Notch, where you will find huge boulders strewn around the landscape and challenging hiking routes leading up to vistas of the mountains. Fishing — especially fly-fishing — is very popular in the creeks and rivers here. If you don't mind the occasional hill, the cycling options in the Lamoille River valley and in the mountains around include everything from graded bike-paths to challenging single-track mountain-biking. There are five golf courses in the area and, if you want a little nightlife, it is just forty-five minutes into the clubs of Burlington. Nightlife at the Mannsview Inn consists of soaking in the hot tub or playing a game of pool on the huge billiards table in the living room with the other guests. The pool table is closed at ten so that the noise of the balls doesn't keep up guests who want an early night.

INN INFO

Mannsview Inn ★ ★ ★
916 VT RT 108 South
Jeffersonville, VT 05464
802-644-8321
1-888-937-6266
Fax: 802-644-2006
www.mannsview.com
RSVP@mannsview.com

RENTALS

Smugglers Notch Canoe Touring
RR#2, Box 4319
Smugglers Notch
VT 05464
1-888-937-6266
Fax: 802-644-2006
www.mannsview.com/canoe

MAPS

Maps are available for sale at Mannsview Inn.

TRAVEL INFO

No air service. Trains via **Amtrak** to Essex Junction 20 miles (32 km) from the inn. Best if travel is done by car.

VERMONT

NEW YORK

Manhattan:
Paddling in the Big Apple

Kayak in Manhattan? In New York City? You've got to be kidding! This is a typical response to the idea of paddling in the Big Apple, but Manhattan is in fact a wonderful paddling destination. The history of New York City is very involved with the waterways that come together here. Ever since European colonists bought Manhattan Island for a handful of beads, this city has been a center of commerce, first for the new English colonies, then for the new country of the United States of America, and now for the entire world. In the past, much of that commerce has depended on access to the water, and it still does.

Paddling in Manhattan is not a naturalist experience; rather it is an urban paddling adventure. There is a lot of boat traffic on the rivers and in the harbor, but the traffic is quite orderly and manageable. Manhattan is an island and offers access to the Hudson River, the East River, the Harlem River, and, through New York Harbor, the Atlantic Ocean. We will focus on paddling the lower stretches of the Hudson River and out into New York Harbor. Access can be a bit tricky and parking is an absolute nightmare, but kayaking in and around Manhattan can be a unique soft paddling destination.

I recommend paddling with the Manhattan Kayak Company on one or several of their tours. They supply all the equipment for anyone on their tours, which avoids any problems you may have with boat storage, water access, or car parking. Paddling with the local guides ensures your safety on the busy waterways. These guides know the area very well and are familiar with the boat traffic patterns as well as the boating rules, both written and unwritten, that apply in New York City.

Many of the immigrants to the United States first came to this harbor with a compulsory stop on Ellis Island to be processed by U.S. Immigration. Paddling out around Ellis Island and out around the Statue of Liberty is a paddle along the waterway of the history of the growth of the United States. Seeing the Manhattan skyline from a kayak gives you a perspective of Manhattan not possible from the streets or anywhere else. You will get a view of Manhattan that is all your own, a perspective unique to kayakers. The waterways around Manhattan are used by boats of every description — huge tankers and container ships leaving the New Jersey industrial shoreline share the water with old top-sail schooners, pleasure yachts, ferries, personal watercraft — and, of course, kayaks. You might think that with all of this water traffic, the paddling here would be dangerous and not much fun at all, but if approached in the right way, Manhattan is certainly an exciting and safe paddling destination.

Paddling a kayak here does require a different approach than paddling in a wilderness area, but the basic skills needed are the same. Since many of the boats using this waterway are very large and cannot see kayakers, the rule here is, stay out of everybody else's way. If you are crossing a main channel, cross at right angles to reduce the amount of time you will be in the path of a freighter or cigar boat. Along the shoreline there is a relatively unused strip of water that is either too shallow or too close to piers to be used by most boat traffic. This is the best area to be in when paddling up or down the Hudson River. In fact, I found paddling here much safer than paddling in many tourist boat meccas on the weekend.

Getting the kayaks ready for a trip at the Manhattan Kayak Company dock.

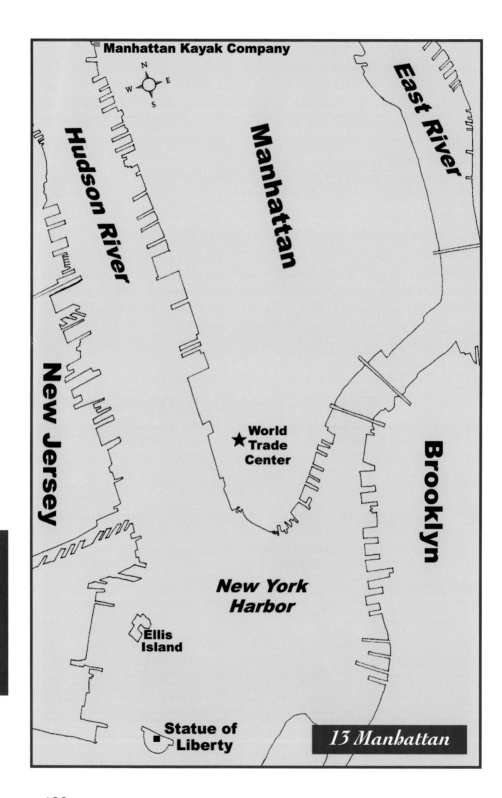

Manhattan Kayak Company

N
W E
S

Hudson River

Manhattan

East River

New Jersey

★ World
Trade
Center

Brooklyn

New York
Harbor

Ellis
Island

Statue of
Liberty

13 Manhattan

NEW YORK

As I mentioned, I recommend paddling with a local guide and using their boats. There are several reasons for this, not the least of which is finding a spot to launch and store your own boat. Public launch sites are very few and far between and have virtually no parking near them. If you come without your own boat, then you can come into the city without a car, which will make your visit to Manhattan far more enjoyable. The Manhattan Kayak Company operates tours from their base on Pier 63 Maritime on the Hudson River. A converted barge with low floating docks attached provides both a space for their kayak storage and a sheltered launch site. This barge also hosts the occasional musical event and serves as a base for a large tour boat as well.

No matter where you go in New York City you will not be far from lots of activity and action. Since 1995 the Manhattan Kayak Company (MKC) has been offering tours and courses in New York Harbor and up the Hudson River. The six owners who operate the trips at MKC all bring a different set of skills and a different approach to their paddling trips. They are all certified paddling instructors, but they each bring a different personality to the water. If you are looking for a specific type of tour, ask which guide will best suit your temperament. From mellow meandering paddles to gung-ho marathon-type tours, this company has something to offer everybody. I was particularly impressed by the way in which MKC will accept anyone at any skill level and work with them on skill development or just on providing a venue for them to experience New York City from the water. MKC also offers a series of courses designed to develop new skills in paddlers from novice to expert.

A few of the tours MKC offer are the Take-off Tour, North/South Tours, Sunset Cruises, Paddle & Pub, 79th Street Boat Basin Café Cruise, Statue of Liberty, Sushi Tour, Verrazano Narrows Bridge Tour — and, to top it all off, a complete Manhattan Island Circumnavigation. They also offer the following courses: Beginner Paddle Basics, Fast Track Paddle Basics, Open River Basics & Rescue Instruction, Advanced Paddle Basics, and a Coastal Kayaking Seminar. While all of the tours start at their Pier 63 dock, some of the courses are not offered in Manhattan. Call first to find out if the course you are looking for is offered in or outside of town.

For those of us who do not live in New York City and even for some who do, the Statue of Liberty tour is a "must-do" trip. This three-to-four-hour paddle around one of the most recognized landmarks in the world encompasses paddling both on the Hudson River and further out into New York Harbor to Liberty Island. It is not possible to land on Liberty Island from a kayak, so if you want to climb the statue or visit Liberty Island you will have to arrive by one of the ferry boats. I did not feel that being prohibited from landing on Liberty Island was a problem on this tour. In

Paddling out to the Statue of Liberty with the Manhattan skyline in the background.

fact, paddling out to the island and watching the statue grow larger and larger with every paddle stroke made the trip far more meaningful than if I had just taken a ferry over to the island with the thousands of other folks who visit the statue every day.

After launching from the float beside the barge at Pier 63 we drifted downstream alongside the newly developed Chelsea Piers. This huge complex seems to contain facilities for every sport known to mankind, and even includes a sub-office of MKC. Over the past few years Manhattan has been redeveloping its waterfront. This waterfront restoration project is slowly creeping up the shoreline from its initial phase around Battery Park. The shoreline between the redeveloped Chelsea Piers and the edge of the waterfront park that is expanding upstream is composed of old piers, decrepit warehouses, and seemingly endless construction zones. Once the waterfront park is expanded north to Chelsea Piers, this paddle will be much more pleasant but perhaps not as historically interesting.

Years ago this was a busy shipping area with freighters and passenger ships lining the docks. When the passenger service died out and shipping moved to other larger facilities, this area of the city became rundown. But now New York is rediscovering its waterfront. On the far bank, the New Jersey shore of the Hudson River is heavily industrialized in this area, but there are a few points of interest. About halfway between Pier 63 and the end of Manhattan Island you will pass what appear to be matched towers rising out of the water close to shore on either side of the river. These towers looking at each other across the width of the Hudson River are air-intake towers for the Holland Tunnel, which carries Interstate 78 into the heart of the city.

In twenty to thirty minutes' paddle past the air towers marking the Holland Tunnel you will be paddling alongside the World Financial Center with the trademark twin towers of the World Trade Center touching the sky behind the glass dome of the atrium in the World Financial Center. The docks in this area are home to some beautiful yachts and a sailing school. The waterfront here has been cleaned up and now has parks, walkways, and a bike path along the shore. Battery Park at the tip of Manhattan is just ahead, and just past Battery Park is the Staten Island Ferry Terminal. The ferries for Liberty Island and Ellis Island leave from a dock in the center of Battery Park's waterfront. It is generally best to cross over to the New Jersey side of the river before you get into the Battery Park area to avoid all of this additional boat traffic.

Ellis Island lies just off the New Jersey shoreline across the main boat channel in the Hudson River entrance from the tip of Manhattan. This island was an immigrant way station from 1892 to 1954. Over twelve million immigrants passed through Ellis Island on their way to becoming new Americans. Once again, it is not possible to land on Ellis Island except from one of the official ferries, but it is an interesting island to paddle around even if you can't land. For anyone whose ancestors passed through the doors of Ellis Island, a trip back on the ferry would be well worth the time. In the main building on the island there is an excellent museum covering the history of Ellis Island and its contribution to the growth of the United States. Ferries to Ellis Island leave from the dock in Battery Park. Tickets can be purchased in the Castle Clinton National Monument.

As you paddle past the southern end of Ellis Island, you will paddle into a shallow area where the water can be very choppy and confused. The tidal currents and the flow of the river combine here to create some very exciting paddling. If you are lucky you may even be able to catch a ride on a couple of waves. If you want to avoid this tricky paddling, stay close to the shore of Ellis Island just past the ferry dock. Be especially careful paddling here since the ferry cannot see you when you are this close to shore. Just past Ellis Island, the shore of New Jersey has been extended with a long stone breakwater. Along the top of this breakwater is a pedestrian trail, where you can get into conversation with the occasional fisherman trying his luck as you paddle alongside these boulders. Contrary to popular belief, the fish this fisherman might catch are considered safe to eat. The past twenty years of environmental awareness and clean-up have resulted in the lifting of the ban on eating almost all species of fish out of New York Harbor. As the river gets healthier and recovers from centuries of abuse, perhaps more and more people in New York will experience it and spend more time on the river in recreational pursuits.

From the New Jersey shore breakwater, it is just a short crossing over to Liberty Island and the Statue of Liberty. This historic and majestic statue was a gift to New York from France. Dedicated in 1886, the statue has hosted millions of visitors and was completely refurbished in 1986. This icon of America, which has been featured in hundreds of movies, loses none of her power when approached by kayak. She seems to stretch ever taller into the sky when seen from the water lapping at her feet. When paddling over from the shelter of the New Jersey shore, keep a close watch out for the Statue of Liberty ferries. They dock on the side of the island that faces New Jersey and are not maneuverable enough to avoid an inattentive kayaker. As you paddle below the rock wall surrounding the island, compare the size of the tourists walking along the wall to the huge statue behind them. When you paddle around the corner of Liberty Island for the return trip to MKC's dock, the entire skyline of Manhattan is laid out in front of you. From the easy-to-spot twin towers of the World Trade Center to the Art Deco needle of the Chrysler Building, the wide range of architectural features in the cityscape of New York City is spread out before you. It is truly a beautiful site, completely unique to this type of kayak trip.

If MKC has timed the trip right, you will be able to ride the incoming tidal current back upriver to Chelasea Piers. Sometimes the tour to Liberty Island includes a stop at a small café in one of the New Jersey boat basins for refreshments and relief for the inevitable call of nature. The trip back upriver, although it is along the same stretch of waterway, seems completely different from the trip out to visit the lady with her torch of liberty. In the distance the river curves around Manhattan Island, lined on both sides with a forest of concrete and steel. Sometimes a huge luxury cruise ship will pass you on its way to or from the Cunard Line passenger ship terminal between Pier 88 and Pier 94. The trip back seems to take far less time than the trip out, perhaps because the tidal current is pushing you. Once back at the MKC dock, it is time to help store the kayaks and get dry clothes on. After all, the rest of New York City is waiting to be explored.

Another tour that I would highly recommend doing while on a paddling trip to New York is a sunset tour. Barring absolutely horrible weather, this paddle is

The Statue of Liberty tour is a must for anyone paddling in New York City.

spectacular even if it is too cloudy or hazy for a good sunset. The lights of Manhattan provide a show regardless of weather.

These are short paddles, taking only a couple of hours, starting just before the sky darkens and finishing at the barge when the city lights have completely outlined the skyline. One particularly hot, hazy June evening, I paddled out on one of these sunset tours. It was more a sun-fading-away tour, but that really didn't matter. The heat in the city was intense but out on the water the temperature went down dramatically.

The tops of the tallest buildings were lost in the low cloud cover and the whole city seemed to be cast in a dusky gray light. The towers of the World Trade Center appeared to be holding up a soft gray ceiling. We paddled south to take advantage of the ebb tide. As the light drained from the sky, the buildings began to sparkle. At first the lights were tentative, a few here, a whole floor of a building there, but as the last shreds of daylight faded away the city seemed to come alive. Whole buildings flashed on like white fire running through the city. Where there had been a gray leaden city there was now a fairyland of light. Even if the city planners had designed this light show, it could not have been more impressive. We drifted along caught up in the moment, wanting to prolong the magic as long as possible. Reluctantly we headed back to the MKC dock and quietly stowed away the kayaks.

I was the only person from outside New York City on that paddle, but I think we were all equally impressed that the city could look so beautiful on such a hot and muggy evening. The love that all New Yorkers seem to hold for their city was certainly confirmed in those paddling residents that night. You can imagine that if the city is that beautiful on a cloudy night how spectacular it is on a clear starry night. These trips are a wonderful way to meet local people who share your interests and sense of adventure. And the best way to explore the rest of the city is also with the advice and help of like-minded people.

There is literally no limit to New York's off-the-water attractions, from taking in the latest Broadway show to wandering the streets of Greenwich Village in search of the perfect bistro. New York City, and more specifically Manhattan Island, is home to hundreds of theaters, restaurants, shopping — and, of course, some of the best museums in the world. There is no point trying to cover here all the activities available to you when you visit New York City. If you have specific interests, ask at your hotel for information.

The hotel I recommend is the Gorham Hotel on 55th Street. It has an unpretentious entrance just across the street from the City Center, and, apart from the lobby, the entire hotel is above street level. It is a delightful boutique-style hotel in the heart of the theater district and just a few blocks from Central Park. The accommodations, decorated in a modern European style, contain luxurious marble baths for post-paddling relaxation. In case you need to bring work with you on your paddling vacation, the Gorham Hotel has the latest in communications hardware installed in every room, from double-line phones to high-speed internet access. Breakfast is served in a pleasant room overlooking the street. Best of all, if you happen to strain some muscles while paddling, the hotel can arrange for a massage therapist to treat you in the its fitness center.

New York City's restaurants are among the best in the world and I would not normally recommend one over the others, but I must mention one very special restaurant. La Bonne Soupe is a delightful little French bistro located just a five-minute walk down 55th Street from the Gorham Hotel, between 5th and 6th Avenue. I had dinner here one evening after a long day of paddling and exploring the city. From the moment you enter, the decor and ambiance make you feel as if you have been transported to a small bistro somewhere in France. And hearing customers and staff speak French among themselves adds to that feeling. The real reason to visit this moderately priced bistro, however, is the almost sublime food. The filet mignon in a creamy cognac and peppercorn sauce is a house specialty, and the French onion soup could be a meal on its own with the wonderful bread that comes from the local French bakery. La Bonne Soupe seems much smaller than it actually is, since it is divided up into several intimate areas, one being a second-floor balcony with just four tables. A large theater crowd frequents this bistro, so you might be wise to make reservations if you plan to arrive before or after a show. On Tuesday evenings an excellent jazz group plays French and American jazz classics.

Manhattan is a wonderful and certainly unique paddling destination. From tricky currents and big water to gentle secluded pools and coastal paddling, there are opportunities for every paddler. It goes without saying that, off the water, there is something for everyone in Manhattan. Indeed, the problem will be to narrow down your choices.

INN INFO

The Gorham Hotel ★ ★ ★ ★
136 West 55th Street
New York, NY 10019
1-800-735-0710
212-245-1800
Fax: 212-582-8332
www.gorhamhotel.com

RESTAURANT

La Bonne Soupe
48 West 55th Street
New York, NY 10019
212-586-7650
Fax: 212-765-6409

MAPS

None needed if you are paddling
with Manhattan Kayak Company
or another kayak company in
New York. You should definitely
paddle with a local guide.

RENTALS

These places do not rent kayaks
but they provide guide services in
which all rentals are included.

Manhattan Kayak Company:
23rd Street and the Hudson River
212-924-1788
www.manhattankayak.net

New York Kayak Co.
The Folding Kayak Specialist
1-800-KAYAK99
212-924-1327
Fax: 212-924-0814
www.nykayak.com

TRAVEL INFO

New York is accessible by train,
bus, plane, and car. But a car is a
liability rather than an asset in
New York City. Parking is
expensive and hard to find, and
it is generally quicker to get
around by transit than by car.

ONTARIO

Gananoque: Thousand Islands Paddling

The Thousand Islands in the St. Lawrence River have been a vacation destination for generations. Rugged granite islands topped with windswept pines appear alongside gentle pastoral islands and mainland farms. The islands themselves are dotted with cottages, some well over a hundred years old. The St. Lawrence Seaway runs through the St. Lawrence River and a network of canals and locks that enable immense ships to bring in goods to the heart of the continent and return heavily laden with manufactured goods and raw materials headed for ports around the world. These ships can take up to 4 miles (6.5 km) to come to a stop, so stay out of their way. The international border between Canada and the United States runs right down the middle of the river. This chapter focuses on the Canadian shore and the islands around Gananoque, Ontario.

Gananoque is a small town that explodes in the summer months. The tourist industry in Gananoque revolves around the St. Lawrence and the islands that are liberally sprinkled throughout the river. From Victoria Day in May until Labor Day thousands of people stream through Gananoque, taking tour boat rides on the river, shopping for antiques, or just extending their visit to Kingston just a few miles upstream. The water is dotted with hundreds of boats on the weekends, but during the week it is possible to find quiet areas to paddle.

Directly offshore from Gananoque are the Admiralty Islands, a group of some seventy islands sandwiched between the Ontario shoreline and Grindstone Island on the American side of the river. Several of these islands have been protected as part of St. Lawrence Islands National Park and have picnic sites and landing areas on them. There is a landing fee on the National Park Islands in the summer months — but there are also bathrooms and sheltered picnic areas. This park was established in 1904 as Canada's first national park east of the Rocky Mountains. At first just a small parcel of waterfront property donated by the Mallory family, it now includes all or part of twenty-four islands and ninety islets, in addition to its large 100-acre (38 hectare) mainland base at Mallorytown Landing.

The St. Lawrence River valley is the meeting place of two distinct ecosystems, the Algonquin region of the Canadian Shield and the Adirondack Dome of New York State. The unique conditions in the river valley have created small pockets of habitat containing flora and fauna normally only found much further south. In the summer you will have to contend with boat traffic and people at most take-out points in the park. But it is possible to paddle here in the spring and fall and see very few boats or people. The park is not the only reason to paddle here, though. In fact there is so much to see paddling here that without visiting even one of the park islands you will still be hard pressed to experience it all in one trip to the area.

The Gananoque River runs through the center of the town of Gananoque, emptying into the St. Lawrence under an old swing bridge. The Gananoque Inn sits on the waterfront between the bridge and the St. Lawrence River. This elegant old inn is a perfect base for a soft paddling adventure in the Thousand Islands area. The Gananoque Inn started out life as a carriage works in the 1870s. When the carriage business was moved to Brockville, the Brockville Carriage Company converted the old factory building and opened the Gananoque Inn in 1896. Since then the inn has operated continuously under different owners.

In 1995 the Keiltys bought the inn and began the process of restoring the "Grand Old Lady" to her former elegance. John Keilty grew up in Gananoque and is passionate about making the Gananoque Inn the best that it can be. The inn offers a modified American plan, which gives you breakfast and dinner in addition to your room, making it possible for you to completely relax and enjoy the paddling. The inn has a small launching spot in its own private harbor and it also rents kayaks. Everything needed for a soft paddling vacation is provided by the inn. All you have to do is show up, although making reservations is a good idea most of the time.

The Admiralty Islands lie a half a mile (1 km) offshore from the docks in front of the inn. The island group gets its name from its many islands named after admirals in the British navy. Further downriver are the Lake Fleet Islands, named after warships of the British fleet. Plan on spending at least a day exploring these islands. If you paddle west along the mainland shoreline, you will be following a main boating channel that leads to the gap between the mainland and Howe Island. A cable ferry crosses the river here at the entrance into Bateau Channel. Turn south and paddle into the islands just a short distance from shore.

The closest island is Beaurivage Island. A lot of it is national parkland, but there are a few secluded cottages on the points. If you continue south through these islands you will pass Aubrey Island, also part of the park system, and then emerge into open water. Looking west from here, you can see out into an open channel between Howe and Wolfe Islands that leads to Kingston, about 10 miles

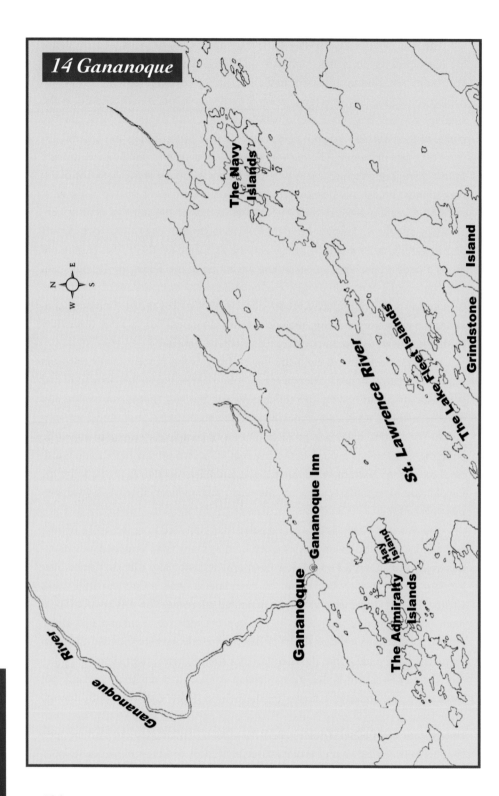

14 Gananoque

The Navy Islands

Grindstone Island

St. Lawrence River

The Lake Fleet Islands

Gananoque Inn

Gananoque

Hay Island

The Admiralty Islands

Gananoque River

(15 km) away. There are often high waves and choppy conditions out here, especially with a west wind. To head back into the islands you could either choose the Wanderer's Channel directly through the middle of the islands or stay on the south shore of Bostwick Island, cutting through the marshy grass between Bostwick and Blackduck Islands.

After Blackduck Island, turn north and look for a narrow entrance to a cove in the shore of Bostwick Island, which is located just north of three smaller islands lying offshore. The entrance of this cove is marked by a large sign in the shape of a sickle moon that reads "Half Moon Bay." Half Moon Bay is a watery chapel — a kind of marine drive-in church. The rock walls of this narrow cove come together at the end in a platform on which there is a simple pulpit. Every Sunday all summer a worship service is held here. The parishioners arrive by boat, moor together in rows, and sit in their boats throughout the service. The rocks and cliff face have metal hooks and cables to moor the boats to. The spot always seems very peaceful and is sheltered from all weather. The land here is private and is maintained by a volunteer every year. Please respect this area as you would any church and leave with some extra tranquility in your heart.

Heading northeast from Half Moon Bay you will pass through the center of the island group past huge, grand island homes and small, quaint cottages. In a half-hour paddle through here you will see cottage styles for every architectural taste and budget, ranging from Victorian to Bavarian to Moorish. At the extreme east of the Admiralty Islands group is Hay Island. Most of Hay Island is part of the national park but a strip along the west and north shores is covered with cottages. The other shores are national park but there is nowhere to land. But what you will find is a huge area of towering marsh grass with small channels leading through it. Once you are into a channel, you are completely cut off from the river, just a narrow strip of water in front of you, and tall grass rising high above your head on either side up to a narrow strip of sky above. Paddling through here, it is easy to forget you are only a mile's (2 km) paddle from the dock at the Gananoque Inn. This marsh is the habitat of hundreds of birds. Spring and fall are great times to paddle here, when migrating waterfowl use this marsh as a refueling station for their long flights.

The last of the Admiralty Islands lie almost due south of Hay Island. The largest of these is called Leek Island on the topographical maps and Thwartway Island by the St. Lawrence Islands National Park, of which it is a part. This is a great destination for sea kayakers because it has a beach, washrooms, and mooring buoys but no docks. This dramatically cuts down on the number of motorboats using this area and allows for a more relaxed island visit. The land just to the south here is not mainland; it is Grindstone Island, part of New York State. The Seaway

Threading our way through the Thousand Islands.

runs on the other side of this island, so to see really large ships you would have to paddle all the way around this island. It is possible to paddle from Gananoque to Clayton, New York, around Grindstone Island, but you would have very little time to look around before heading back in order to make the round trip in one day. I would not recommend this to any but the strongest paddlers.

From Thwartway/Leek Island, Gananoque is a 3-to-4-mile (5–6 km) paddle north. If you are lucky you may be piped into the small harbor in front of the inn. When we returned from paddling through the Admiralty Islands, the sounds of a bagpipe wafted across the water. At first, we didn't know where it was coming from but it got clearer the closer we got to the Gananoque Inn. We got our answer when we turned into the inn harbor and saw a bagpiper walking slowly up and down the wharf sending music out across the water. What a great way to end a day on the water! After a shower and change, it is time to sit down to a delicious meal looking out over the river. The chefs at the Gananoque Inn turn out superb meals that you can enjoy either inside in the dining room or on the adjoining patio overlooking the tiny harbor where you just landed.

If you are looking for a change from paddling on the bigger water of the St. Lawrence River, then consider paddling up the Gananoque River to the dam at Marble Rock. This is a full daytrip in which you are more likely to see other paddlers than motorboats. The one thing lacking on this trip is any place to stop and pull out on the trip up and back. Most of the shoreline is private and much of it has no place to land. Apart from the lack of rest spots, paddling this river is a wonderful way to spend a day in a kayak or canoe.

Start the day by getting the inn to shuttle you and your boats to the put-in upstream of the pond with the fountain in it in the center of town. From the old railway bridge, which is now a recreation trail bridge, there are no portages until you reach the dam at Marble Rock 7.5 miles (12 km) upstream. The first section of the river is wide and placid. Some days you will see members of the local canoe club racing their tippy craft north and south on this section of the river. As you leave the town behind, the roar of Highway 401 ahead becomes more audible. If it weren't for the noise of the highway, this section of the river would seem quite wild. Highway 401 crosses the river on a huge concrete bridge high above the water. Dozens of swallows live under this bridge seemingly inured to the constant noise.

As you paddle north of the 401 bridge, the noise slowly dissipates and finally fades away altogether when you round a bend in the river. The river here is very slow moving, more like a long narrow lake than a river, but when it turns north a little further ahead its character changes. A small stream runs into the river from the west with a large swamp near the junction. There is also an island near this point that has a small rock extending into the water at the northern end. It is possible to stop here for a bit, but this is also private land so keep within 10 feet of the water if you do land.

Paddling north from this junction you will be passing through a favorite local fishing hole. The marshy shoreline provides a home for many different types of birds as well as muskrats — and thousands of frogs. I have never seen such a concentration of frogs anywhere before. When you paddle around another bend you will see first a road by the side of the river and then a railway bridge running over the river. Homes lining the road on the east side of the river have lawns that continue on the other side of the road right down to the river. There are often Canada geese in this area. There is some inexplicable attraction between closely trimmed grass and Canada geese.

The west side of the river is overgrown farmland with sandy banks. Where the road crosses the river a bit further north, you pass through the hamlet of Maple Grove. The shoreline becomes wooded on both sides of the river for the next half-mile (1 km), and then slowly breaks up on the west shore into pasture and scrubby fields. The west shore continues to become more developed as you paddle north, with farms and small homes set well back from the river. The east shore becomes much more rugged and its tall trees and dense woods rise steeply from the river. Slowly the east shore becomes less rugged, and just south of Marble Rock another road crosses the river.

It is only a half a mile (1 km) from the bridge to the dam and rapids below it, but the topography changes a great deal in that distance. The river becomes squeezed between high hills on both sides and the current increases. The best spot to land before the dam is on the east side of the river. There is a small landing area and, above it, a clearing obviously used as a party spot. A rough trail leads over a bit of land and eventually takes you back to the river on the north side of the falls. It is best to ignore this trail, though, and make your way out onto the rocks lining the riverbank just below the dam. The rapids here and the water rushing over the dam will quickly make you forget the clearing behind you. North of here the river turns into a huge swamp and eventually reaches Lake Gananoque. Don't portage to the north side of the dam unless you have lots of time to get back to Gananoque. It is 7.5 miles (12 km) back to the take-out and it seems to get longer the closer you get.

The return trip is helped somewhat by the current. I am always amazed at how different a river looks when traveled in the opposite direction. Just after we paddled under Highway 401 we started to feel as if there was nothing more to see. Then we paddled around a corner and saw a deer standing by the water framed by the leaves behind her. As we stopped paddling to watch her, she turned her huge liquid eyes on us, stared at us for a couple of minutes, and then slowly ambled into the trees. We were very close to our take-out point, and yet we felt as if we were in the wilderness.

There are several other paddling options in this area. How much you want to do will depend on how long you want to spend in your kayak. Just downstream from the Admiralty Islands lie the Lake Fleet Islands, and just past them are the Navy Islands. It is possible to cut through the Admiralty Islands to the western end of the Lake Fleet Islands and then follow them east downriver. When you reach Sugar Island you must decide whether to keep going for another 5 or 6 miles (8–10 km) or cut north to Gordon Island and then follow the Ontario shoreline back to Gananoque.

It is a long paddle back from the Navy Islands, especially with the prevailing west wind. Just exploring the Lake Fleet Islands can easily take another day, and as mentioned earlier it is possible to visit Clayton, New York, by kayak if you are up for a long haul. Another gentler and more pastoral paddle would be to Johnson Bay, west along the Bateau Channel between Howe Island and the mainland. Once you pass the cable ferry cutting across the entrance into the channel, the shoreline is very unpopulated, especially on the Howe Island side. In a stiff west wind this would be a difficult paddle, but I highly recommend it under normal weather conditions.

When you want a break from paddling or if the weather just won't let you out on the water, the Thousand Islands area has many other activities to offer you. For a change of pace, there are 40 miles (64 km) of bike trails along the river. Bikes can be rented at the inn or in town. There are four golf clubs close by, and of course there is that other on-the-water sport, fishing. The Thousand Islands are known through out the world as a great fishing destination, and the Gananoque Inn has contacts with several local fishing guides who will happily show you where to catch the "Big One." On a more cultural note, the Thousand Islands Playhouse is just a half a block from the inn. This superb summer theater group performs four or five plays every season in a converted old canoe club.

History buffs will love the St. Lawrence valley. From the huge limestone battlements of Old Fort Henry in Kingston to the reconstructed Upper Canada Pioneer Village, there are enough historical sites and museums to satisfy anyone who is interested in the unique history of this area.

Gananoque

INN INFO
The Gananoque Inn ★ ★ ★ ★
550 Stone Street South
Gananoque, ON
K7G 2A8
613-382-2165
Fax: 613-382-7912
1-800-465-3101
www.gananoqueinn.com
ganinn@gananoqueinn.com

OTHER ACCOMMODATIONS
Misty Isles Lodge
(Camping and Cottages)
613-382-4232
www.mistyisles.on.ca

RENTALS
Available through the
Gananoque Inn

MAPS
Canadian NTS Maps, 1:50,000,
Gananoque 31 C/8

TRAVEL INFO
Accessible by train and air.
Highway 401 takes car travelers
directly to Gananoque,
20 minutes east of Kingston.

VIA RAIL SERVICE
1-888-VIA-RAIL
www.viarail.ca

AIR SERVICE
1000 Island Air
613-382-7111

Escape from Toronto:
The Briars on Lake Simcoe

L ake Simcoe is an almost circular expanse of water measuring 18.5 miles (29 km) by 14 miles (25 km) just north of Toronto. Lake Simcoe was named by Lord Simcoe after his father, but it had many names before that. To the local Natives this lake was "Place of the Dog Call," and the early French fur traders called it Lac Toronto, which means "gateway" or "pass." Champlain marked it on his maps as Lac aux Claies or Lake of the Stakes, later shortened to La Clie. The shallow water and wide open expanses of water have kept Lake Simcoe free of some of the boat traffic problems that beset many lakes further north. Although only an hour from Toronto, much of the lake is quiet most of the time, and the paddling options here are wonderful.

Lake Simcoe is bordered on the south by sandy beaches, sheltered coves, and the Briars. The Briars is an inn and manor house surrounded by gardens, towering trees, and stately lawns right on the water's edge. It offers golf, tennis, sailing, and mountain biking in addition to kayaking. A full-service spa in the main inn is available for you to work out any aches and pains you may develop on your paddling trips. The high central tower of the Briars acts as an excellent homing beacon for finding your way back from a day on the water.

The Sibbald Family has been operating the Briars since they purchased it in the 1870s, first as a gentleman's farm and later as a resort. The golf course was opened in 1924 and came under the leadership of the Sibbalds in 1942 as the Briars Golf and Country Club. As time went on, more and more energy was focused on the resort and less on the family home. In 1977 the main inn was opened in the newly renovated and expanded family home. A stay at the Briars includes all accommodations, meals, and canoe or kayak use. They even grow some of the vegetables for the table right on site. You have absolutely no worries except how you want to spend your day.

The Briars has managed to blend the various eras and styles of these buildings into a cohesive and pleasant whole. As you wander through the grounds on your way to and from dinner or the indoor swimming pool or the spa, try to picture where various building were joined and imagine their previous functions. One of the more interesting buildings is an elaborate octagonal brick structure between the main inn entrance and the gardens. This beautiful brick building is a peacock house.

Paddling here is simply a matter of walking down to the waterfront and launching into Lake Simcoe. The Briars has both canoes and sit-on-top kayaks for your use here. If you want to paddle a more traditional sea kayak with a skirt you must bring your own. And if you do bring your own kayak, you can store it with their boats while you are a guest at the resort. There are three main paddling areas accessible from the Briars: west along the shore of Briars Bay and around Jackson's Point to the shoreline dotted with estate homes, east along the shore to Sibbald Point and out to Georgina Island, and inland up the Black River into the town of Sutton. Each area has its own advantages.

Paddling west around Jackson's Point will take you by the harbor here. There can be a lot of boat traffic in and out of this harbor on weekends and even on weekdays after four in the afternoon. This is the home of Grew Boats, now makers of mostly aluminum and steel motorboats. But they used to make one of the most beautiful lapstrake catboats in Ontario. These pretty boats look much like the famous Aykroyd day-sailers, partly because Grew got his training under Aykroyd.

There is a small rocky beach near the mouth of the harbor just west of the breakwater where it is possible to land and stretch your muscles. As you paddle around the long sloping curve of the western side of Jackson's Point, Snake Island will come into view in the distance. Like all the islands in this part of Lake Simcoe, Snake Island is part of the Georgina Island Indian Reserve, and is private property. It does make for an excellent turn-around point, however.

About halfway between Jackson's Point and Snake Island is Willow Beach Conservation Area. There is a good landing area here at the end of the beach, and there are washrooms just up the hill. It is also a great place to go for a swim if you are getting overheated. The water here is quite shallow with a sandy bottom, so it is one of the warmer parts of the lake to swim in. The shallowness of the water also contributes to the formation of fairly steep waves that can build up very quickly in a west or northwest wind. One of the real advantages of paddling west is that you will likely have a following wind on your return to the Briars.

Paddling east to Sibbald Point Provincial Park and then across to Georgina Island is a much longer trip than heading west. Count on spending an entire day, especially if you plan to paddle all the way around Georgina Island. This island is part of the territory of the Chippewa of Georgina Island First Nation. The channel between the island and the mainland is very shallow, and steep, close waves can build up in this area. There is a small chain of islands partway across that will give you a bit of shelter, but be careful of the weather when paddling out here.

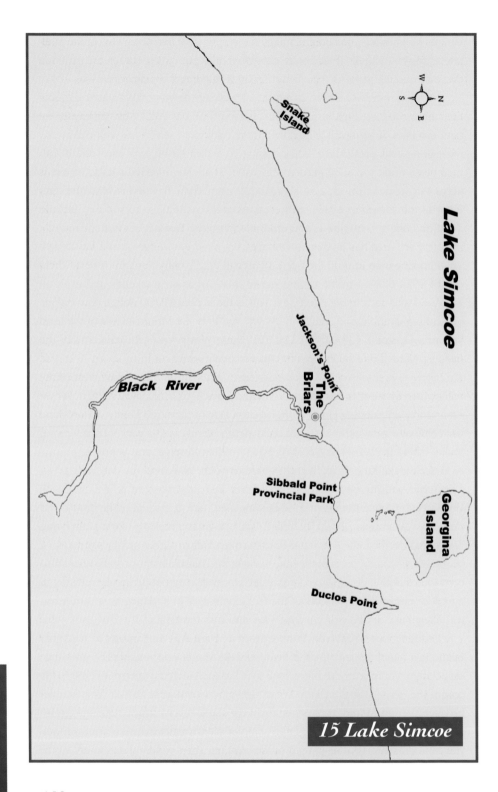

Snake Island

Lake Simcoe

Jackson's Point

The Briars

Black River

Sibbald Point
Provincial Park

Georgina Island

Duclos Point

15 Lake Simcoe

Once out along the shore of Georgina Island there is nowhere to run for shelter, so if the sky looks threatening, do not paddle out around the island. Sibbald Point Provincial Park has a good landing area and beaches and picnic facilities as well as washrooms, if you want to take a break. The return paddle to the inn from the east can be tiring since the prevailing westerly winds tend to build up over the day and are strongest in late afternoon.

If the winds are too high and the waves too big, or if you just want a tranquil day paddle, head inland along the Black River. The Black River winds inland from its mouth in Briars Bay. A long breakwater extends from the river mouth, and the water on the western side of the channel can be quite shallow. This is a great spot to practice your surf technique if the waves are high enough. It is also an excellent canoe daytrip. It feels good to change from a kayak to a canoe every once in a while, use different muscle groups, and sit in a different position.

Birdwatchers and wildlife lovers will definitely want to paddle this river. The first hour of paddling will take you through the Briars golf course. The only hazard you might encounter on this river would from misdirected golf balls. The bridge between the tenth and eleventh hole is completely covered in climbing vines that are home to many birds. As the golf course falls behind, the shoreline becomes wilder. There are occasional pockets where homes back on the water and boats are tied up to docks, but overall the river becomes more and more quiet. There is an old boathouse with just part of its roof still standing, and the shoreline is being reclaimed by the woods.

There are many turtles along this stretch of the river, and the dragonfly population seems to be particularly strong here. We stopped to look at three turtles all lined up in a row on a log, and when we picked up our paddles again there were dozens of dragonflies of different shapes and colors resting in the sun on our kayak decks and paddles. We identified at least seven different birds in one short stretch on the water. One of the reasons for the abundant wildlife here is that this river is a protected fish habitat. Fishing is not allowed in the river and there are signs posted all along the river to this effect.

When you arrive in Sutton, your way will be blocked by a high dam across the river. A road crosses the river on a bridge right above the dam, making a nice shady spot to get out of the sun. On the eastern bank there is a public access point where you can get out of your boats and lock them up so that you can wander around the town. The access take-out is a 2-foot-high concrete wharf that can be a bit of a challenge to get onto from a kayak. A little patience and careful maneuvering will see you safely onshore. The trip back down the river will take a bit less time than the trip up as you will be going downstream, but there is very little current in the

*The tall tower of the main building at the Briars makes an excellent homing beacon
at the end of a day on the water.*

ONTARIO

142

summer and fall, so count on an almost equal time to return. You don't want to miss a great dinner at the Briars.

If you prefer not to take a whole day to paddle on one of the above trips, consider just paddling around off the main waterfront area. The waves that build up here with a good west wind, and the shallow warm water make this an excellent place to work on improving your paddling skills.

Once off the water there are many activities to keep you busy near the Briars. The Red Barn Theatre, located in the old Briars barn, is the oldest operating professional summer theater in Canada. Check with the front desk about what shows are playing and for reservations. Just down the road at Sibbald's Point is St. George's Church. This beautiful stone church was built by the Sibbald family in memory of their mother Susan Sibbald in 1877. It is a great destination for a short bike ride from the Briars. Golfers will certainly have noticed the 18-hole golf course run by the resort. Check with the front desk for tee-off times. A stroll through the extensive gardens and the butterfly garden is refreshing at any time. You could also play tennis or try your hand at croquet. Finally, just walking around the 50 acres (20 hectares) of grounds or soaking up the tranquility under a pine tree on the front lawn is a perfect way to relax.

Lake Simcoe

INN INFO
THE BRIARS ★ ★ ★ ★ ★
55 Hedge Road, R.R. 1
Jackson's Point, ON
L0E 1L0
905-722-3271
Fax: 905-722-9698
416-493-2173
1-800-465-2376
www.briars.ca

RENTALS
Not needed, but if you want a
true sea kayak, rentals are
available in Toronto.

MAPS
Canadian NTS Maps, 1:50,000,
Beaverton 31/D6

TRAVEL INFO
One hour by car from Toronto
The area is served by GO Transit
bus service.

Lake Rosseau: Unwinding at Windermere House

Paddling up to Windermere House on Lake Rosseau in Muskoka, you feel as if you are in the early twentieth century. The hotel silhouetted against the sky looks much the same as it did 75 years ago, and the landscape around it has changed little in the 130 years since Windermere House first took in paying guests. This is an illusion, however. The hotel sitting so proudly on the shore like one of the grand old hotels is in fact only a few years old. Construction was finished in 1997 when Windermere House opened its doors for business — again — like a phoenix rising from the ashes, stronger and more beautiful than before. Windermere House has recovered from a tragic fire that completely destroyed the old hotel in the winter of 1996. It is amazing that less than a year after the fire the hotel had been completely rebuilt and was back in business.

Those who have visited Windermere House over the years notice hardly any changes from the original appearance of the hotel, but under the seemingly antique facade, there is now a very modern hotel. When the decision was made to rebuild, the Windermere Company decided to ensure that the character of the hotel remained unchanged. They chose architect Joseph Sibbald to design the new hotel from the ashes of the old. The original stonework of the verandah was all that was left of the old hotel and it was seamlessly incorporated into the reconstruction. Many new materials were used in the reconstruction; the siding is not wooden clapboard but a cement-based siding that is far more fireproof. The framing on the main floor is steel, and there is now an elevator for better access to the upper floors. When you stay at Windermere House, you may be in a new building but the spirit is definitely that of the grand old Lady of the Lake.

One of the highlights of staying at Windermere House is the dining experience. The food is unique, drawing on traditional foods such as venison and local cheeses, which are exquisitely prepared. We always made sure we were back to the Windermere House well before dinnertime in order to prepare for dinner. Savoring this cuisine in the Arts and Crafts dining room after a day on the lake is an experience reminiscent of an earlier gracious era.

Lake Rosseau has been attracting summer visitors for well over a century. This landscape that is so hard to farm is ideal for recreation. The hard granite of the Canadian Shield had no industrial uses other than lumbering, so the local settlers turned to providing an escape for people who wanted to get away from the increasingly polluted cities and back into nature. By the 1890s, tourism was replacing lumbering as the main economic force in the Muskokas. Lake Rosseau and Windermere House were at the forefront of this tourism boom.

Two transportation achievements made it possible for the resorts here to be economically viable. The first was the railway line into Gravenhurst, and second was the launching of several steamboats on the Muskoka Lakes. Lift locks between the lakes gave quite large vessels access to all the main lakes. These steamships supplied the resorts on Lake Rosseau with large numbers of guests, most of whom would stay for at least a month, if not the whole season. The beautifully restored HMS *Segwun*, still sailing out of nearby Port Carling, offers summer visitors the chance to experience Muskoka by steamship. Sometimes the *Segwun* still calls at the Windermere dock.

Today most of us cannot afford (or take the time) to spend the entire summer on Lake Rosseau, but Windermere House is a delightful place to spend a few days while exploring the lake by canoe or kayak. A sea kayak will allow you to widen your range, but you must bring your own. Canoes are available from the recreation staff at Windermere House and are the more traditional craft used here.

Paddling on Lake Rosseau offers a wide variety of experiences. There are quiet backwaters, islands to thread through, built-up areas, and almost wild areas. There are big open water stretches and literally miles and miles of water to paddle with no portages. So it is ironic that one of my favorite paddles in this area involves a portage. Clark Pond and the Dee River provide a near-wilderness paddling experience close to the hotel. The main item lacking for paddlers on Lake Rosseau is public landing areas. It is legal to land at Clark Falls.

Paddle north along the shoreline past some beautiful big cottages. These are more waterside mansions than cottages, with large boathouses, outbuildings, and landscaped grounds. One of my favorite ones has shingled gables. Each row of shingles is a slightly different color so the whole gable looks like a slice of a prism. It is only a mile and a half (3 km) up the shoreline from Windermere House to Clark Falls, but it can take quite a while to paddle if you look at all of the cottages.

Clark Falls tumbles down through a slanting granite channel in the rock. There is a portage on the north side of the falls. It is hard to imagine now that this site was once a busy lumber mill and the village around the mill was larger than Windermere Village. The mill burned down in 1929, and the village was slowly reclaimed by the forest. Clark Pond was created by the dam and it now provides a

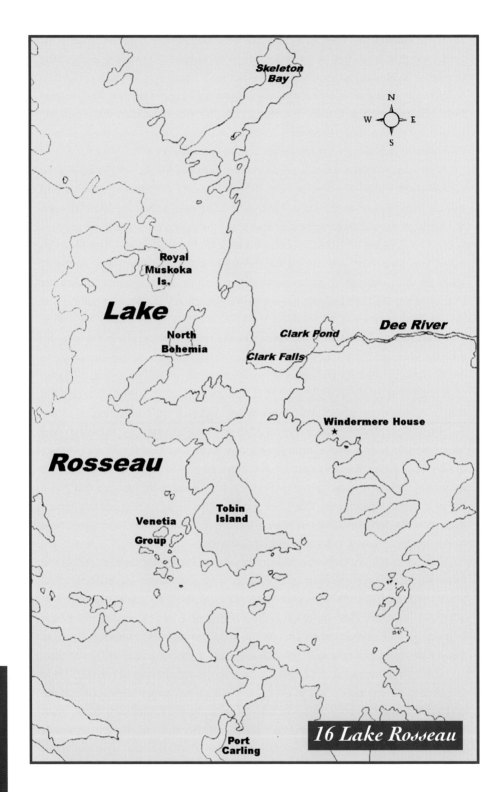

Skeleton Bay

N
W — E
S

Royal Muskoka Is.

Lake

North Bohemia

Clark Pond

Dee River

Clark Falls

Windermere House
★

Rosseau

Tobin Island

Venetia Group

Port Carling

16 Lake Rosseau

tranquil paddling spot close to Lake Rosseau. The fishing here is supposed to be very good — just floating around the lake pretending to fish would be a great way to spend a day.

On the far side of Clark Pond is the Dee River. This slow meandering river runs from Three Mile Lake (actually 3 kilometers) upstream. The first mile (2 km) is beautiful with trees overhanging the river on both sides. Further upstream, just past a bridge, the land has been cleared and you paddle out into bright sunlight. The trees return to the riverside for a bit before you reach another bridge. This is a good spot to turn around since the current gets a bit stronger and there are two rapids up ahead. The trip back downriver with the current pulling you along goes far more quickly than the paddle upstream. The falls is a good spot to stop for lunch.

After a day spent exploring Clark Falls, Clark Pond, and the Dee River, you may be looking for a bit more strenuous paddling the next day. A good full-day paddle is the circumnavigation of Tobin Island with a side trip into Port Carling for lunch. Or if you want to make it a shorter paddle and give yourself more time to explore Port Carling, paddle into Port Carling around the southern tip of Tobin Island and then return along the east shore of Lake Rosseau. If you do plan a paddle around Tobin Island, head north first so you have a shorter distance on the return from Port Carling.

Two deep bays cut into Tobin Island from the east: Snowshoe Bay and John's Bay. You can cut across the mouth of each of these if you want to take a shorter time, but I like heading into them to drift along the shoreline looking at the local flora and fauna. Once you round the northern end of Tobin Island, you will be more exposed to open water and the waves that go with it. Halfway down the west side of the island, Barn Bay reaches into Tobin Island, almost joining up with Snowshoe Bay on the far side.

Straight ahead is the Venetia Islands Group. When paddling through here keep an eye out for Hideaway Island. It is joined to St. Leonards Island and Zurich Island by footbridges. Woodmere Island is joined to the mainland by a narrow spit of land and a footbridge. The first point past Woodmere Island is Oaklands Point, and the entrance to the channel leading into Port Carling is directly south of here. The channel winds its way around Lakeview Park Island, so it is almost impossible to see it from the north. There are channel markers leading into the channel as well, since this is the main route between Lake Rosseau and Lake Muskoka. It is from this connection between the lakes that Port Carling gets the nickname "Hub of the Lakes."

If you are lucky the Muskoka Lakes Association Antique Boat Show will be happening when you get into town. Port Carling hosts this show on even-numbered years and it is a pilgrimage for old-boat lovers. Another place to visit when you are in Port Carling is the Township of Muskoka Lakes Museum, located on the island

Clark Falls is an excellent place for a lunch break while paddling Lake Rosseau.

between the two locks. There is at least one restaurant in Port Carling right on the water where you can paddle up to the dock, tie up or pull out your canoe and have lunch. The docks of the Green Slate Inn are about a quarter of a mile (500 m) to the northwest of the lock entrance. The return paddle to Windermere House takes about an hour and a half around the southern end of Tobin Island.

If you are looking for a longer paddle, the trip north through open water to Rosseau Village is a good full day-trip. Paddle north as if you were going to Clark Falls and then continue past the falls between North Bohemia Island and the mainland. A short jog around the point in front of you — inaccurately called an island (Royal Muskoka Island) — and you will be able to see 5 miles (8 km) north to the village of Rosseau. This is a long paddle and, with a west wind funneling down the lake, it can be a lot of hard work. On the point to the east as you paddle into the small bay by the village is Lake Rosseau College. This private school was once the Eaton estate on Lake Rosseau. Little remains of the original estate buildings due to fire and renovations, but it still is one of the best sites on the lake. Although this is a long paddle in a canoe, if you have brought your own kayak it is a nice daytrip in a sea kayak. It is over 13 miles (20 km) round-trip from Windermere to Rosseau village.

Muskoka abounds in off-the-water activities. Windermere House offers tennis, golf, and swimming, and further afield there are miles of roads to bicycle. Steamships still ply the waters of the Muskoka Lakes. Sometimes they even still call in at the Windermere dock. For further information on these historic boats, talk to the staff at the front desk. Algonquin Park and Georgian Bay are both less than an hour away by car, and there are many museums and visitor centers in Algonquin Park.

Lake Rosseau

INN INFO
Windermere House ★ ★ ★ ★ ★
Windermere, ON
P0B 1P0
705-769-3611
Fax: 705-769-2168
1-888-946-3376
www.windermerehouse.com
info@windermerehouse.com

RENTALS
Not needed. Canoes are supplied at the resort.

MAPS
Canadian NTS Maps, 1:50,000, Lake Joseph 31 E/4

TRAVEL INFO
Easiest access by car. Small float planes and regular shuttle flight service from Toronto. No bus or train service.

Stoney Lake:
Captivated by the Kawarthas

North of Peterborough and Lindsay in Ontario there is a group of interconnected lakes called the Kawartha Lakes. The name Kawartha comes from the Ojibwa phrase *ka-wa-tha*, meaning "bright waters and happy lands"— a very fitting name for this area know mostly as a summer cottage destination. The queen of this lake system is Stoney Lake.

Stoney Lake is a long, narrow body of water with beautiful scenery and great paddling. The lake bed is the meeting place of the granite rocks of the Canadian Shield to the north and the limestone shelves and glacial till of good and gentle farmland to the south. Although 9 miles (15 km) long (more if you include Clear Lake running down to Young's Point), Stoney Lake is only a little over a mile (2 km) wide at its widest point. Over 1,100 granite islands covered in woods dominated by twisted white pines are strewn throughout the lake. These islands provide shelter from winds and make paddling the lake an exploratory adventure every time. It is almost always impossible to see your destination until just before you reach it.

The best soft paddling accommodation on Stoney Lake will be found at Viamede Resort. Viamede translates from Latin as "by way of the middle." Viamede Resort is located in the middle of the north shore of Stoney Lake and has been offering rooms to vacationers since Colonel Sam Strickland opened the inn here in 1870. The original building was destroyed by fire in 1907 but rebuilt by 1909 and has continued through various renovations and additions to improve the service and luxury that are the hallmarks of this inn. The Viamede Resort offers canoes and kayaks for your use, so all you need to bring with you is your clothing and your love of adventure.

Because of the central location of Viamede Resort, you are perfectly positioned to explore the lake in three directions. Each of the following daytrips is of a different length. I will start with the longest and work down to the shortest. Canoe trips up Eels Creek to High Falls have been part of summer life on Stoney Lake for generations. This trip offers a chance to get away from cottages and motorboats, and ends at a beautiful waterfall. It is a long paddle, about 10 miles (16 km) round-trip with a couple of short portages, so make sure you give yourself lots of time.

From the beach, head southeast across the bay toward the channel between Anchorage Island and the mainland. The cottage on this point is an architectural marvel: the glass and steel of the upper story seem to float above the lower earth-bermed story. Several sculptures dot the grounds and a large rock has been placed near the shore to make a natural diving board. This is not a small, rustic cottage! Once past the point, you head east through the islands. Northey's Bay will open up on the north shore once you get through the first group of islands. From the point after Northey's Bay, paddle straight east through the next group of islands. There is a temptation to paddle along the north shore here but if you do, it will greatly increase the overall distance you need to travel.

Another open stretch of water allows you a chance to align your bow with the gap between the mainland and Simpson Island. If you follow the north shore after this point, it will slowly curve north into the mouth of Eels Creek. Right at the point where Eels Creek flushes into the Stoney Lake, there is a spot that requires a short lift-over. A short paddle past this lift-over and you will be confronted by a short rapid locally known as Suicide Cut. Portage around on the right side and continue paddling upriver under the bridge. As you paddle upstream, there are two swifts, points at which it may be necessary to get out and either portage or simply walk your canoe up through the fast water. Sometimes when the water is high you can paddle up through these sections. The last one of these swifts will take you into a large round pond. Just on the other side of this pond is High Falls. Paddle across the pond, keeping close to the west shore. Another channel will open up in front of you, and you will see an obvious take-out spot on the east bank.

The roar of the falls fills the air. A trail over the rocks will take you to the top of the falls where there are plenty of places for a picnic. If you are going to swim here, be very careful of the current. It is quite powerful near the top. You might enjoy a shower in the lower falls if the water level is not too high. But wear shoes or good sandals in the water here. I have seen several broken bottles in the water here left by inconsiderate party-goers. A trail from this site leads to Petroglyphs Provincial Park, but as it takes a minimum of four and a half hours to walk the full route, I would not recommend trying to hike in.

Your return trip down Eels Creek to Stoney Lake will be speeded up by the current. Be careful not to be swept over Suicide Cut! Depending on the water level, you may be able to float down the other two carry-over spots. The paddle back to Viamede can be very enjoyable as long as there is not a west wind. West winds are the prevailing winds here and a strong west wind will make the return paddle an exercise in finding the right islands to shelter behind, followed by quick sprints

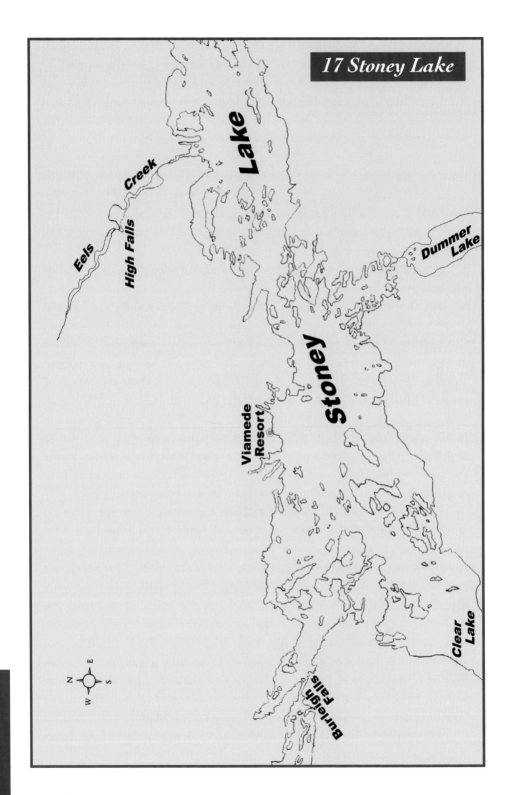

17 Stoney Lake

Lake

Eels Creek

High Falls

Dummer Lake

Stoney

Viamede Resort

Clear Lake

Burleigh Falls

N E S W

across open water to the shelter of the next island. Fortunately there are enough bays and islands between Eels Creek and the final point near Viamede Resort that it is possible to paddle almost the entire way in shelter. The last half-mile (1 km) from the point into the beach at Viamede Resort is wide open and can be a real tough but exhilarating end to your trip.

When you decide to head west from the resort, you will immediately find yourself threading your way through dozens of islands and barely submerged rocks. I love looking at the names of these islands on a map and trying to figure out the stories of the more colorful ones. Some obviously come from the people who built the cottages — Knapmans Island, Stubbs Island, Clark Island or Robinsons Island, for example. But what about some of the other names? Plum Pudding Rock, Fiji Island, Hurricane Point, Devil's Elbow Passage, Hell's Gate, and Elephant Rock evoke images of stories related to these places. Did someone lose a plum pudding on Plum Pudding Rock or does it just look like a plum pudding? If you happen to pass one of the local residents on their dock you might ask them about these names. I have asked many times of many different people and received almost as many answers, but I will keep asking because the stories are always entertaining. Your goal on this day's paddle is Burleigh Falls, a small village and site of one of the locks on the Trent-Severn Waterway.

For the last mile (2 km) of paddling you will be in or alongside the Trent Canal route, so be careful of large boats. Try to stay close to the sides of the channel, because the deep part of the channel is not very wide, and larger boats have very little room to maneuver. As you paddle up to the falls, you will notice a cove on the south shore from which most of the water is flowing. At the head of this cove is a 3-foot (1 m) waterfall, and to the side is a spot to pull out your canoe. Be careful of the currents and watch for swimmers as you paddle in here. You can leave your canoe off to the side in the parking area here. This is a great place to go swimming, and just across the main road is a restaurant where you can get lunch.

One of the best parts about this trip is the possibility of a tailwind to push you back to Viamede Resort. The north shore about halfway between Burleigh Falls and Viamede is very swampy and is an excellent spot to look for herons and other waterfowl. Generally there are dozens of redwing blackbirds here as well.

The third trip, setting off in the southeast direction across the lake from Viamede, will bring you to Gilchrist Bay and the entrance to Dummer Lake. This paddle requires one short portage around the Gilchrist Bay dam, but it takes you off Stoney Lake onto a completely different lake with a much different topography. Where Stoney Lake is dotted with islands, Dummer Lake has only a few at the northern end. Stoney Lake has lots of cottages that seem to be spaced well apart, but the cottages on Dummer Lake line the shore like houses in a subdivision.

A paddle up Eels Creek takes you into a near-wilderness setting.

Dummer Lake is the headwaters of the Indian River and flows south into Rice Lake through the Warsaw Caves both above and below ground.

From Viamede, start out as if you were going to High Falls. From the first point of land, it is a straight shot across the wide-open water of the lake to Black Rock, an island at the mouth of Gilchrist Bay. Threading your way through the islands, you will come out on an open section of the bay. In the southeast corner of the bay is a small inlet leading to the Gilchrist Bay Dam. A short portage around the dam will get you into the quarter-mile (500 m) stretch of the Indian River that leads into Dummer Lake. Three islands and a few well-marked rocks cover the entrance to Dummer Lake. Once past these islands, it is slightly over a mile (2 km) to the end of the lake and the entrance to the Indian River. Water levels in the river fluctuate a great deal; sometimes it is possible to get a good distance downstream and sometimes you will be stopped a short way into the river. Regardless of how far you get, it feels like an adventure. The return to Viamede Resort is just a simple retracing of your steps.

There are several other paddling options in this area. The really energetic could paddle to Young's Point at the bottom end of Clear Lake for lunch. Clear Lake is a southern extension of Stoney Lake that starts after the group of islands to the southwest of Viamede. These islands themselves make for great exploring; check out the old and new cottages. Some of these are over a hundred years old and some are new this year. Juniper Island is a small community on the island of the same name. The Stoney Lake community has a church on an island, a sailing club, and recreation center . . . and a full social calendar. Many of the cottagers who spend their summers on the lake are descendants of the original cottage owners. The summer regatta is still a big social event. If you are lucky, you may be on the lake at the right time to see the sailing, canoeing, and other races of this regatta.

If you want a break from paddling, Viamede Resort offers many other activities. They have great mountain biking, horseback riding (including a horseback trip to High Falls), archery, waterskiing, and, of course, just sitting by the water relaxing. You must not miss the Petroglyphs Provincial Park just a short drive away. The "Teaching Rock" here has dozens of ancient Native petroglyphs chiseled into the crystalline limestone rock. Most of the petroglyphs are now sheltered in a huge steel-and-glass building in order to preserve them from the effects of acid rain — and, more important, to protect them from vandalism. South of Stoney Lake is Warsaw Caves Conservation Area. As long as you don't mind getting a bit muddy, you might enjoy exploring these water-sculpted caves with the aid of a good flashlight. Last but definitely not least, Peterborough — just a thirty-minute drive from the resort — is home to the Canadian Canoe Museum. This museum has the largest collection of canoes in the world, including ancient dugouts, voyageur birchbark canoes, modern cedar and canvas canoes, as well as Inuit kayaks. Any canoe lover will want to spend several hours here.

INN INFO

Viamede Resort ★ ★ ★ ★
General Delivery
Woodview, ON
K0L 3E0
705-654-3344 or 1-800-461-1946
Fax: 705-654-4749
www.viamede.com
E-mail: viamede@kawartha.com

MAP

Canadian NTS Maps, 1:50,000,
Burleigh Falls 31 D/9

RENTALS

Not needed, but sea kayaks can
be rented at:

Adventure Fitness
County Road 18
R.R. # 3
Lakefield, ON
K0L 2H0
705-652-7986 or 705-652-7041
Fax: 705-652-7986

Wild Rock Outfitters
167 Charlotte Street
Peterborough, ON
K9J 2T7
705-745-9133
1-888-945-3762
www.wildrock.com

TRAVEL INFO

Car access only.

Algonquin Park: Back to Nature at Bartlett Lodge

lgonquin Park. The name is synonymous with wilderness and paddling. Most people who come to Algonquin for more than a day spend at least some time in a canoe. Algonquin became a provincial park in 1893, the first in Ontario and one of the largest in all of Canada. For many, Algonquin Park's main attraction is its large network of canoe routes with maintained portages and marked campsites. Although camping is generally a part of the Algonquin experience for most people now, it was not always this way. In the period between 1920 and 1950 many lodges in Algonquin offered comfortable accommodations in the heart of the forest. Some of these could only be reached by boat, adding to their appeal for vacationers from the city.

Only three lodges still operate in Algonquin Park — Arowhon Pines Hotel, Killarney Lodge, and Bartlett Lodge — and only Bartlett Lodge, the oldest, is still approached by boat. At the landing and parking area on the north shore of Cache Lake, you pick up the telephone on the side of the small waiting shed by the dock. It rings across the water in the office of Bartlett Lodge, and very soon you will see a large motorized freight canoe approaching the dock to pick you up. This short boat ride across Cache Lake, which takes you into a different world, makes the Bartlett Lodge experience unique. The staff at Bartlett Lodge will shuttle you back and forth across the lake to the landing given a few minutes' notice at almost anytime of the day.

The lodge is a jumble of unobtrusive buildings clustered on the shore of Cache Lake. If you have ever been to summer camp, you will feel as if you are returning as soon as you arrive at the dock. But all memories of roughing it in the woods vanish once you enter your cabin. Although you are in the center of Algonquin Park, you will be pampered here. The rooms border on the luxurious, and the view from your window across the tranquil lake inspires serenity. Only the haunting call of a loon or the hoot of an owl is likely to disturb your sleep. Bartlett Lodge provides both breakfast and dinner in the dining room — again with little resemblance to summer camp meals. Many summer residents of Algonquin Park make a regular

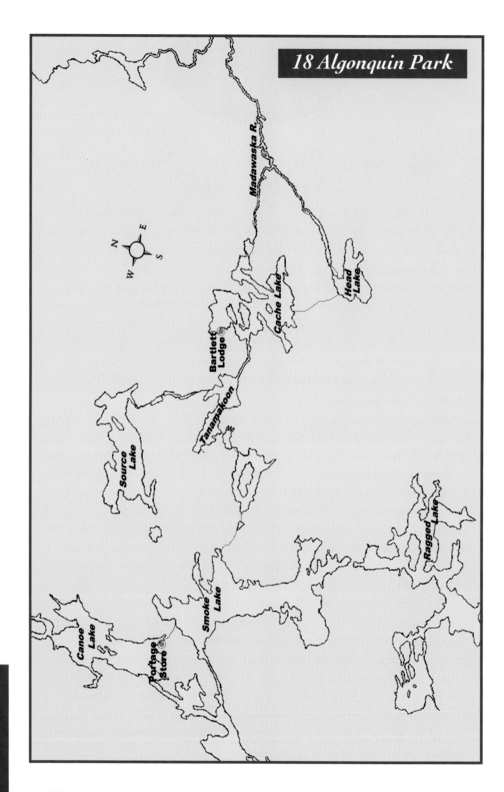

18 Algonquin Park

Madawaska R.

Head Lake

Cache Lake

Bartlett Lodge

Tanamakoon

Source Lake

Ragged Lake

Smoke Lake

Canoe Lake

Portage Store

pilgrimage to the tables of Bartlett Lodge to enjoy the cuisine here. The food is presented in an elegant manner that would do justice to a posh city hotel. A combination of pampering, indulgence, and escape to nature is what a soft paddling trip here is all about.

Canoeing is the preferred method of transportation in Algonquin, and Bartlett Lodge provides canoes for your use. Just go to the front desk and pick a paddle and lifejacket — or bring your own, and select a canoe from the dock. Most paddling trips from here will take a full day, so make plans to bring a picnic lunch or to have lunch at your turn-around point. I will cover two daytrips here, one to the Portage Store on Canoe Lake for lunch, and the second into a more remote wilderness area to the south on the Head Lake/Makawaska River loop. On both these trips, you will really appreciate soft paddling, as you will not be carrying the usual camping gear and food packs over the portages.

To paddle to Canoe Lake and back, start at the docks of Bartlett Lodge and paddle south following the west shoreline. You will pass some of the many cottages on Cache Lake on the first part of this paddle. About half a mile (1 km) south, you will come to the entrance of a channel leading west to Tanamakoon Lake. Follow the channel into the lake and head for the buildings on the far shoreline. This is Camp Tanamakoon, a girls' camp run by the owners of Bartlett Lodge. If you follow the south shore on the side of the lake away from the camp you will shorten your paddle a bit. Just past the camp, the south shore drops away to form a bay. At the foot of this bay is your first portage, 135 yards (120 m) around a dam.

Many of the dams in Algonquin were built by lumber companies to create better waterways to float their logs to the mills. Most of these dams are now kept up by the park in order to maintain the present canoe-route system. The end of this portage will put you on Sheriff Pond. A short paddle directly across the pond, and you are at the second portage, an easy 350 yards (320 m) into Little Island Lake. As its name implies, Little Island Lake is dominated by an island that takes up most of the lake, leaving a wide channel all the way around it. Paddling the north side is slightly shorter than taking the south shore.

At the end of the island, the mainland shoreline comes out in a peninsula. On the south side of the peninsula there is a deep bay with a portage at the foot of it. This 240-yard (220 m) portage will take you into a small pond, Kootchie Lake, on the far side of which is the longest portage of the day, a 900-yard (830 m) sometimes muddy trail that crosses into Smoke Lake. Paddle north for a mile and a half (3 km), and you will arrive at the public ramp and docks at the north end of Smoke Lake. Smoke Lake is a large lake for Algonquin and it can sometimes be quite windy. If the weather looks at all threatening, keep close to shore.

Along the shores of Smoke Lake there are many cottages, some with boats moored to their docks and almost all with a canoe either flipped over on the dock or stored on a rack close to the dock. Although motorboats with limited horsepower are allowed on Smoke Lake, the canoe still reigns here. If you are just going for lunch at the Canoe Lake Portage Store, you can leave your canoe at the Smoke Lake dock and walk across the busy portage — really just the side of road — to the Portage Store. This is one of the busiest places in Algonquin, so be prepared to meet people both on the walk to the store and in the store itself. There is a restaurant on the upper level of the store overlooking the beach that is the most frequent start- and end-point for interior canoe trips.

From your table, you will see canoeists of every skill level paddling by on the water below. There will be first-timers experimenting with how to make their canoe go in a straight line, guides from the camps up the lake soloing in a fast arrow-straight course, and returning canoe-trippers, their clothes various shades of mud-gray, looking hungry and in need of a shower, but very, very happy. After lunch it is time to head back to your canoe and paddle the route back to the Bartlett Lodge. Make sure you leave in plenty of time to get back before dinner so you can clean off the mud and grime from your own canoe trip.

For a shorter trip with a bit more portaging and a far more remote feel, try the Head Lake/ Madawaska River loop. This trip starts with a paddle to the extreme south end of Cache Lake to the start of an 1,800-yard (1,640 m) portage into Head Lake. Check the sign at the portage to make sure that you are on the trail to Head Lake and not Hilliard Lake. The Hilliard Lake portage is one bay to the west of the Head Lake portage and, although it is much shorter, it leads to many more long portages. The Cache to Head Lake Portage is fairly flat and if you take your time and take breaks as you need them it does not seem to take very long. It is like a walk in the woods, and except for a few muddy spots it is a very well-kept portage trail. There are canoe rests fastened between trees at about 6 feet off the ground at intervals along the trail. These bars are for the portager to rest a canoe on from a solo carrying position without having to flip it down and then up again. Take the time to enjoy this trail as it passes over a ridge of land and then gently descends to the quiet waters of Head Lake. Head Lake is just as likely to be visited by hikers as it is by canoeists. The Highlands Backpacking Trail runs along the northeastern edge of the lake, and there are several campsites along the trail beside the lake.

Your time on the lake is quite short, however. Paddle less than a quarter of a mile (500 m) from the portage landing along the north shore of the lake, and you will come to the outlet of Head Creek. There you will find a short 275-yard (250 m) portage around a set of falls that marks the transition from the lake into the creek.

Seeing loons up close is one of the benefits of paddling in Algonquin Park.

This is a beautiful portage and a great place to stop and explore a bit, especially in the fall. The light slanting through the golden and brilliant red leaves strikes the waterfalls, turning the spray to golden mist. In the spring, there can be more than the usual number of blackflies here, but in late summer and fall this is a choice spot for a snack or lunch.

After this portage, Head Creek is quite slow and placid for about a mile (2 km), until you reach a short 165-yard (150 m) portage. The next area of the creek is a great place for spotting moose, so be very quiet when you enter the water after this portage. Herons, mallards, buffleheads, mergansers and many other types of birds can be seen along this creek. After the next portage, 135 yards (120 m) over muddy terrain, Head Creek connects up with the Madawaska River. It can be difficult to find the channel to take here, but as long as you look for current in the water you will be okay.

Turn upstream into the current to travel back up the Madawaska to Cache Lake. After a very grassy marsh section, the river current becomes stronger and an old railway embankment becomes visible on the north side of the river. This is now part of the trail system that runs all the way east to Whitefish Lake and joins up with the Highlands Backpacking Trail. The trail veers away north from the river, and to the south huge granite cliffs rise out of the water. I have not seen any peregrine falcons here but it seems like a habitat they would like. Further upstream a portage sign comes into view. This 210-yard (190 m) portage ends at a footbridge across the river.

The trail across the bridge leads to the forestry tower overlooking Cache Lake. It is about a one-mile (2 km) round-trip hike to the tower from the bridge, and you are about an hour and a half from Bartlett Lodge at this point. Give yourself lots of time, since you do not know what the water conditions will be like on Cache Lake when you get out on the open water. A head wind there can slow you down considerably. From the put-in by the bridge it is a short paddle to the next and last portage. Just before a small falls you will find the start of a 400-yard (360 m) portage leading into Cache Lake. Be careful when crossing this portage that you do not make a wrong turn. The forestry tower trail crosses this trail, and it might be possible to take the wrong turn if you are not paying attention.

From the launch point at the end of this portage you will see a decrepit railway trestle running out into the lake. Follow the direction of the trestle until after it crosses a point of land. Just past the point of land, the railway line again crosses the water, but the trestle is even more decrepit here than before. In the middle of the span, there is a gap that marks your route south down a long narrow channel. At the end of this channel on the right-hand point, you will pass by the tents and cabins of Northway Wendigo Camp. Compare the rough living that these campers enjoy for the summer to the luxury awaiting you at the Bartlett Lodge. Zigzag your way back up through the islands of Cache Lake to the lodge, a hot shower and a much-needed dinner.

If day-long trips and portaging are not to your taste, it can be quite enjoyable to spend a day paddling the shorelines of Cache Lake and its sister Tanamakoon Lake without once portaging. It is a great place to try out that new sea kayak, to practice your solo paddling skills, or to just float on a calm lake under a full moon and listen to the loons or wolf howls. No matter how you paddle in Algonquin Park, it will take you back to nature and relaxation.

The Highway 60 corridor through the park has several museums, art galleries, and a big visitor center in which to spend a rainy day. It is also very pleasant to just relax with a good book on your porch at Bartlett Lodge and listen to the patter of the raindrops on the roof overhead. For mountain bikers, the Minnesing Mountain Bike Trail offers very challenging single-track touring on loops of varying lengths and difficulties. For an easier ride, the Old Railway Bike Trail runs along the old railbed, the railbed you paddled by on the Madawaska River. But by far the second-most popular way to explore Algonquin Park after canoeing is hiking. There are dozens of hiking trails and interpretive trails both long and short within a short drive of the Cache Lake landing.

INN INFO

Bartlett Lodge ★ ★ ★ ★
Summer Address:
Algonquin Park, P.O. Box 10004
Huntsville, ON
P1H 2G8
705-633-5543
Fax: 705-633-5746

Winter Address:
297 Lakeshore Road East, Suite 2
Oakville, ON
L6J 1J3
905-338-8908
Fax: 905-338-3039
www.bartlettlodge.com
E-mail: bartlett@globalserve.net

RENTALS

Not needed but if you don't want
to paddle to Canoe Lake you can
drive there and rent a canoe from
the Portage Store to explore
Canoe Lake, Smoke Lake and
Tea Lake. For the routes
discribed in the text you can use
the canoes available at Bartlett
Lodge.

MAPS

Canoe Routes of Algonquin Park
by the Friends of Algonquin Park

*Algonquin 1: Corridor North: The
Adventure Map* by Chrismar
Mapping Services

TRAVEL INFO

No trains, buses, or planes. Car
access only.

Acknowledgments

Writing this book would not have been possible without the assistance of many people. The owners and staff of the inns and bed-and-breakfasts mentioned in the text made this book possible by creating such wonderful places to stay so close to great paddling destinations. We spent a lot of time far from home while doing the research for this book, and many people befriended us and made us feel welcome in their homes.

My parents have been an immense support to me throughout my life and gave me the sense of freedom and support that allows me to travel and write.

A special thanks to all the people we met who helped us in our research: Missy Campbell, for being a great paddling partner in Mystic and Block Island; Julia Grand, for paddling the Lamoille River and sharing her knowledge of Lake Champlain; all the folks at the Manhattan Kayak Company; Jolyn Clark, for trying out paddling in Chatham and for being such a good sport about being photographed; Gayle McBride, for keeping us interested in the Thousand Islands area; Stephen, Karen, Nicholas and Megan Beamish, for paddling with us on Lake Rosseau; and all the others who paddled with us for a day or an hour and made our time on the water so special.

We would also like to thank the people at Boston Mills Press for giving us the opportunity to write this book.

Finally, we would like to thank Dagger, Cascade Designs, Werner Paddles, Navarro, Five Ten, Fuji and Harmony for their support. It would have been hard to write this book without the support of all of these people. Thank you all.

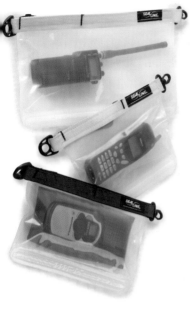
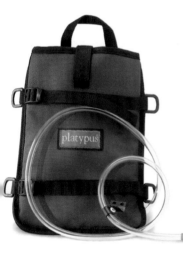

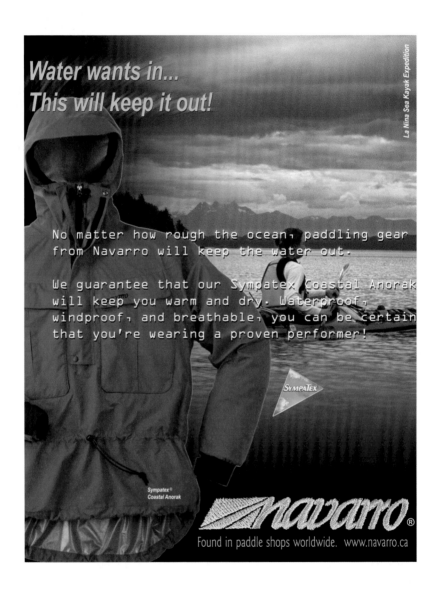

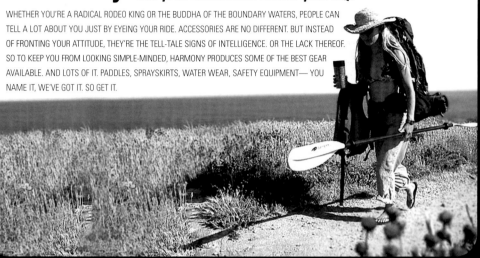
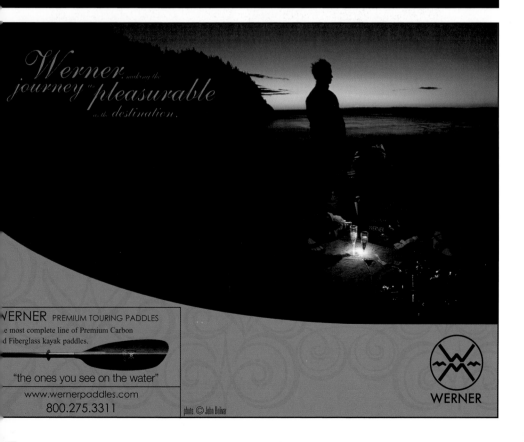